ZOMBIES
OF THE WORLD
A Field Guide to the Undead

ZOMBIES
OF THE WORLD
A Field Guide to the Undead

ROSS PAYTON

Andrews McMeel
PUBLISHING®

Preface

This book comes from two loves of mine: zombies and nonfiction books on fictional topics. Zombies fascinate us, but far too many people see them only as props for their own survivalist daydreams and fantasies. They relish devising plans to survive a zombie apocalypse and playing video games in which they splatter countless undead miscreants with excessive firepower. However, the most fascinating aspect of the zombie is its inability to starve. It is the perpetual motion machine of the horror genre. A rotting, brain-eating perpetual motion machine, to be sure, but a perpetual motion machine nonetheless. What scientist wouldn't spend a career reverse engineering this secret for the betterment of all mankind? They would study the undead and write books about them. Not just dense tomes of scientific argot but introductory primers on zombies to educate the public. I grew up reading similar books. *Bulfinch's Mythology* and the Dungeons & Dragons Monster Manuals explained in minute detail the genealogy, behavior, and social organization of impossible creatures. Of course, in those books, these creatures existed mostly to be killed by heroes, which is quite taboo in today's society. Rare and endangered creatures need to be protected, even if they are lethal. Zombies shouldn't be treated any differently than Siberian tigers. With these thoughts in mind, I wrote this book.

Acknowledgments

This book would not be possible without the help of my parents, Leland and Crystal. My brother, Strader, supported me more than he wants anyone to know. I love you, Maddy, with all my heart. Special thanks to John Margolies, whose work proves books are still valid. I cannot thank the artists enough: Tom Rhodes, Ean Moody, Violet Kirk, Bryant Koshu, and Myriam Bloom. Thanks to James Knevitt for editing this book. I also want to thank all of my friends who put up with my endless discussions of zombie minutiae, especially Tom Church, Patrick and Karee Williams, Chris Farmer, Diana Botsford, Cody and Samantha Walker, Jason Ariciu, and Nathan Shelton. Thanks to all the listeners of my podcast *Role Playing Public Radio* as well.

Andrews McMeel Publishing
a division of Andrews McMeel Universal
1130 Walnut Street, Kansas City, Missouri 64106

www.andrewsmcmeel.com

20 21 22 23 24 SDB 10 9 8 7 6 5 4 3 2 1
ISBN: 978-1-5248-5883-4
Library of Congress Control Number: 2019950507

Editor: Katie Gould
Designer: Sierra S. Stanton
Production Editor: Elizabeth A. Garcia
Production Manager: Cliff Koehler

Illustrators: Tom Rhodes (cover and pages 3, 12, 17-18, 27-66, 87-88, 93, and 108), Violet Kirk (pages 2, 19-21, and 68-77), Ean Moody (pages 15, 94, 97, and 101), Myriam Bloom (page 81), and Bryant Koshu (pages 104-105, 107, and 110)

ATTENTION: SCHOOLS AND BUSINESSES

Andrews McMeel books are available at quantity discounts with bulk purchase for educational, business, or sales promotional use. For information, please e-mail the Andrews McMeel Publishing Special Sales Department: specialsales@amuniversal.com.

Contents

INTRODUCTION

The zombie was ancient even when the ziggurats of Mesopotamia were but the idle dreams of priests and masons. They predate even the earliest records of their attacks, cave drawings of Neolithic hunters. Recently unearthed evidence suggests that our ancestors *Homo habilis* were preyed upon by proto-ghouls, although we do not know if they are related to the modern *Mortifera* species. The history of humanity is incomplete without taking the undead into account.

They have tirelessly trudged in our footsteps, forever at our backs, arms outstretched. They are a reminder of our mortality and, in the eyes of many, proof of the supernatural. But this is not so. The gaze of science and reason has uncovered many secrets of the zombie, proof that they are as natural as you or I. But the greatest questions have yet to be answered: where did they come from? How does their internal biology work? What can we learn from them? So far we have only teased a few tidbits out from the cold, hard grip of the zombies, but even these few samples have staggering implications. Cures for diseases, an end to all zombie attacks, and even a new source of clean and renewable energy are all possibilities.

Researchers around the world work on these mysteries every day, having a global conversation about the zombie. Biologists study how zombies reproduce and migrate. Physicists try to figure out how the undead remain animate without any apparent food source. The field of zombie studies is diverse, covering not only the hard sciences but the social sciences and humanities as well. Sociologists record the effects of zombies on human society. Linguists have made great strides in learning how to communicate with the undead. Historians piece together the story of the zombie.

Every new mind, new perspective adds to this conversation and this is where this humble book and you come into the picture. *Zombies of the World* will only show you where the conversation has been going, not where it will lead. The path to enlightenment is a long and meandering road. But every journey begins with a single shuffling step. Let this book be that first step.

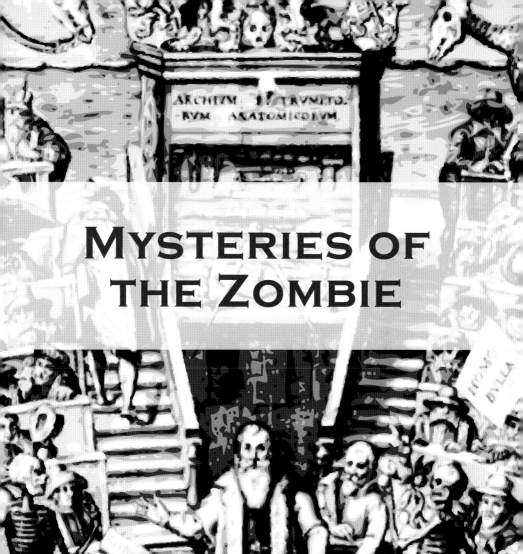

Mysteries of
the Zombie

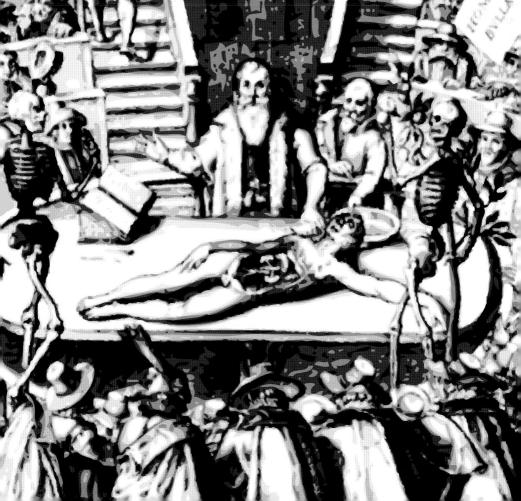

Project RESURRECTIONIST: modernizing research

As with many parasitic and symbiotic species, the reproductive cycle of the zombie involves other species, primarily humans. Many zombie species reproduce by infecting humans through physical contact, typically a bite. So, at what point does an infected human become a zombie and why do we classify them as a separate species? Before 1968 these questions were not asked. The state of zombie research was poor, as only a scattered hodgepodge of knowledge had been recorded in disparate fields of study. No one used a comprehensive interdisciplinary approach to zombie research.

Until 1968, zombies were not recognized as a species but rather as a cluster of poorly understood diseases with such names as African rabies, Wesker's disease, or Rage Flu. They were poorly understood because cases were rare, isolated, and poorly documented. Most literature consisted of sensationalist accounts that lacked proper academic rigor. But in 1968, the North American Zombie Awakening swept across the country. The US government initially believed that the USSR was behind it. Mobilizing the entire strength of the US military-industrial complex to learn the truth of the matter, hundreds of biologists, doctors, chemists, and other experts captured thousands of zombies for study in a project code-named RESURRECTIONIST. While most of the captured specimens were Common Gray Shamblers, they also found zombies with highly differentiated traits, such as Mary, a Dancing Zombie (*Mortifera immortalis choreographicus*) who performed the twist, or Thomas, a New England Ghoul (*Mortifera immortalis pickmani*) who was actually intelligent enough to converse with interviewers. Such examples were the first physical proof that the Victorian-era celebrity "Melmoth the Wanderer" was in fact a ghoul and not a human in costume, as previously believed.

Right: A declassified Project RESURRECTIONIST document. The entire project was shrouded in mystery until portions were declassified in the late 1990s. Some portions will not be declassified until 2068.

These discoveries threw the scientific community into chaos. It was clear that the old disease model was an inadequate framework to accommodate the new data, as many of the newly found specimens did not infect humans at all. But no one could agree on a new model that would fit the data. For months, brains behind RESURRECTIONIST debated day and night on the issue, until the team found a common thread linking each of the zombies: the *Omega Anima*, as first mentioned by Dr. Herbert West.

NANRI (North American Necrological Research Institute) Advisory Panel

Central Intelligence Agency

From: Director of Central Intelligence Agency (RES-1)

RES-2
RES-3
RES-4
RES-5
RES-6
RES-7

ef: Project ASTYANAX
Project ICARUS
Project TROJAN

In the context of recent developments, it has become necessary to evalu nd establish a definitive set of protocols with regards to LAZARUS category pecimens, both in the lab and the wild. ~~████████████████████~~ To this nd, project code-named RESURRECTIONIST will oversee a series of experiments nd field tests in order to fulfill the agenda set by the White House. These irectives must be carried out in a timely manner, requiring cooperation from ll involved agencies. All agencies are coded as RES-1 through RES-7 and will e referred to as such in internal documentation. ~~████████████~~ Please review the responsibilities and duties set for your agency nd submit your comments regarding them no later than October 13. The full nd complete participation of all involved agencies is critical to the success f this project. ~~████████████████████~~ RESURRECTIONIST has een deemed a project vital to national security by the White House, and all appropriate resources will be allocated to ensure its continuance.

ABSTRACT: In order to summarize the material covered in the West lectures (recovered from ~~████████████████~~) regarding the Omega Anima theory, it must be remembered that it was ~~████~~ who pushed the Air Force into developing applicable guidelines for using LAZARUS specimens as aircraft ordnance. ~~████████████████████████████████~~. This work is the foundation of all current RESURRECTIONIST protocols. All agencies should use the Von ~~████~~ guidelines as their starting point.

Omega Anima: The great mystery of the zombie

Consider the Common Gray Shambler, *Mortifera immortalis romeroi*. It is a relentless predator of humanity, *Homo sapiens*, and will go to any lengths to consume our flesh. However, its digestive system is inoperative. Its body cannot transform the pound of flesh in its rotting stomach into energy, fuel for the hunt. Yet, it marches on, never resting, never stopping in its hunt. Any student of biological thermodynamics will tell you that all creatures must get energy from some source in order to act. Given that the common zombie exists until destroyed (the oldest Gray Shambler on record is 298 years old) and does not digest food to convert it to caloric energy, where does their energy come from? In order to understand the zombie, one must first understand this, the greatest mystery of our times.

In 1913, famed researcher Dr. Herbert West coined the term *Omega Anima* to label this mysterious power source. Since then, we have learned much about the *Omega Anima*, such as the GHUL genetic markers that all zombie species have in common, tying them all to this source. Unfortunately, no one has been able to discover what the *Omega Anima* is or why it has led to such a variety of zombie species, from the Common Gray Shambler to exotic species such as the Preta or Draugr. The *Omega Anima* appears to produce unlimited energy. Zombies expend tremendous amounts of energy moving their corpse bodies, as their decaying systems operate more inefficiently than a living human. One researcher calculated that a Common Gray Shambler expends approximately 400 calories worth of energy in order to walk a single kilometer. Yet, they walk endlessly until slain. Once the secret of the *Omega Anima* is cracked, the possibilities are endless: immortality, endless clean energy, and more. It may take decades or even centuries before we truly understand this phenomenon. It is not a form of radiation, solar energy, or any other energy that we are able to observe. It seems to appear out of nothingness. Some scientists have even seen zombie cells that appeared to be on the verge of cell death when they swelled with energy without a discernible energy source. In fact, all we can say with authority is that the *Omega Anima* is real, as every other possible explanation does not fit the current data.

The first Undead Studies Conference in 1970 set forth the rules for establishing a new species of undead, using the *Omega Anima* as a commonality between species. All zombies are classified under the phylum *Corpus:*

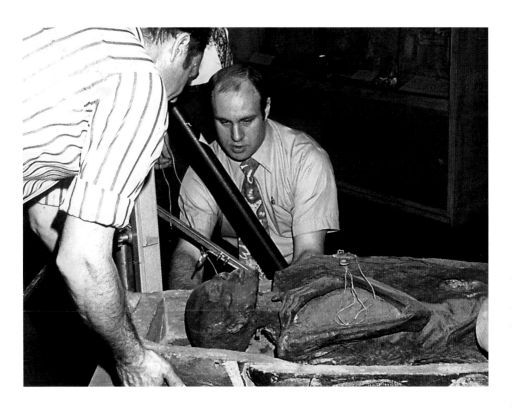

Above: Researchers examine the body of a deceased Egyptian Mummy at the 1970 Undead Studies Conference.

1. The zombie is a parasitic species. All zombies require the corpse of an animal for a host body.

2. The zombie uses the *Omega Anima* for energy, requiring no food in order to remain animate. It may consume flesh, but no species eats enough meat to account for its energy output.

3. The zombie modifies its host body, creating the GHUL genetic markers in its DNA.

This definition has served the scientific community well, holding up under decades of new research and insight. The UN has recognized this definition in several international treaties.

The world's premier zombie-focused scientific think tank, the North American Necrological Research Institute (NANRI), has spent decades trying to determine the origins of the *Omega Anima*. As you will read, it has made many great strides in the field, including the world's first Mummy Sign Language program and a sanctuary for endangered undead species.

Origin of the Species

Despite the best efforts of scholars, we may never know for certain when the first true zombies arose. Certainly they have been around longer than civilization or even the earliest hunter-gatherer tribes of the Paleolithic era. However, *Homo sapiens* is over 200,000 years old. Did zombies begin with us or did they appear even earlier? Some have conjectured about zombie dinosaurs marauding millions of years ago, but this seems more a flight of fancy than a reasonable hypothesis. So-called proto-ghouls have been discovered – fossilized *Homo habilis* specimens with extended claws and fangs similar in nature to several species of undead. However, these proto-ghouls are not considered true zombies. DNA tests conducted on the dismembered finger of a proto-ghoul found in amber in 1993 proved that it lacked the GHUL DNA markers.

Unfortunately, it is simply impossible to conclusively prove whether the oldest known suspected specimens are human or zombie remains, as they are little more than fossilized bones. Once fossilization of a skeleton begins, it destroys whatever trace biological elements that separate *Mortifera* from *Homo sapiens* as we currently understand them.

Above: It is believed that early zombies found North America by following the first human settlers across the Bering Strait.

While several naturally preserved corpses have been found in peat bogs, glaciers, and the like, they are all less than 10,000 years old, well within the known time frame of the zombie. Still, by piecing together the available evidence and filling in the blanks through detailed analysis of the evolutionary process, most researchers believe that viral necrogenesis theory is the most accurate zombie origin theory.

The necrogenesis theory suggests the first zombie arose from an ancient and mutated virus, flawed and unable to reproduce normally. The early proto-ghouls are examples of what the flawed virus may have created. Somehow, this flawed virus tapped into the *Omega Anima*, which gave it the strength to reproduce at an exponential rate. As evolution took its course, the virus changed to utilize the *Omega Anima* as much as possible, using it to overcome the immune systems of any host animal it infected. However, the virus killed the host animal before it could spread so it used the limitless power of the *Omega Anima* to modify the host animal's corpse, bringing it back to life as a zombie so it could infect more animals. This is but the barest of explanations of an immensely complex subject. To adequately describe the theory, readers are directed towards Heidi Von Junzt's excellent primer on the subject *Birth from Death: The Necrogenesis Theory*.

It should be noted that the viral necrogenesis theory is not universally accepted. Some species of undead do not reproduce through viral infection. For example, the Revenant is created only when a person is unjustly murdered and arises from the dead to seek revenge. There is no transmission of a virus from an existing Revenant to the murder victim, so there can be no infection. The fact that Revenants are created because of concepts like justice indicate there is an unknown factor in zombie reproduction that modern science has yet to identify. Still, the viral necrogenesis theory has been useful in research connected to species that do infect humans through viral transmission, such as the Common Gray Shambler and the English Foaming Zombie.

Ultimately, the story behind the origin of the zombie will probably never be fully explained, at least until the *Omega Anima* is adequately understood. The zombie seems to have existed at least as long as we have and perhaps even longer. It is possible that even the dinosaurs had to contend with the undead. We just don't know. But we do know that the undead are here to stay.

Symbiotic relationship with humanity

While zombie animals have been found, such as the endangered Irish Mad Cow, the vast majority of zombie species use humans as hosts. After extensive studies, NANRI published a paper in 1984 that has since been widely accepted as the "Sapience & *Omega Anima* Interconnection Theory." Simply put, it states that the diverse speciation of human zombies is due to the one unique feature that separates humanity from the rest of the animal kingdom: our self-awareness and intelligence.

Consider the Revenant (*Mortifera reverto voorheesi*). It spontaneously arises in a certain percentage of murder victims whose deaths are not punished adequately. As concepts like justice and revenge are artificial social constructs, it stands to reason that the intelligence of the human somehow imprints itself on the nascent zombie, making it a Revenant instead of a Common Gray Shambler. Many other species also show signs of incorporating cultural traits and mannerisms specific to humanity.

Evolutionary biologists have struggled in vain to explain why the traits of certain species are the way they are. The dances of the Dancing Zombie certainly do not help it catch prey or evade predators. In fact, many Dancing Zombies are destroyed by frightened humans even though they are perhaps the most harmless species of zombie in existence. Evolutionary theory would suggest that this species should be extinct because of its inability to adapt to the threat posed by humans. Yet, they survive and seem compelled to show off the freshest moves to every panicked human they can find.

NANRI has recently launched a bold new program, Zombie Cultural Studies, to bring more attention to the intersection between culture and zombies. The program has enlisted the help of top scholars in the social sciences and humanities. Anthropologists and sociologists conduct research on human/zombie interaction. Literary scholars examine historical texts for previously undetected references to zombies. Psychologists and other behavioral experts have made great strides in understanding the psyche of various undead species. Hopefully by better understanding the specifics of how human civilization has influenced the undead and how the undead have influenced us, we can gain new insight into human-zombie relations and communication.

Right: Nonprofit organizations like the North American Necrological Research Institute (NANRI) face an uphill battle in raising funds to protect zombies. Because of the stigma associated with the undead, few people want to donate, so NANRI spends a great deal of time trying to educate potential donors about the importance of its work with brochures, such as this one.

Help Us Help the Undead!

Our Work

NANRI needs your help more than ever with our vital and important work. Donate now to ensure we can continue studying and protecting the undead. We have made great strides in the last few years.

- Created an Undead Sanctuary for rare and endangered zombies.

- Developed the first Mummy Sign Language program.

- Lobbied Congress for better laws to protect the undead and increase federal funding of zombie research.

Mummy Sign Language Breakthrough!

Dr. Linda Hasting has recently revived a dormant Egyptian Mummy through a tanna leaf lotion rejuvenation program. Once revived, Dr. Hasting taught the mummy American Sign Language and has begun to learn many things about how the undead view the world. The mummy, nicknamed Freedom, is quite talkative, so to speak. It has revealed a wealth of information about ancient Egypt and the worldview of the undead. Dr. Hasting believes that her work could eventually be applied to other species of undead.

A Species Gone Forever - The Extinct Aztec Mummy

These are images of the last known Aztec Mummy fighting its natural predator, a temporally displaced robot. They are from a film shot in 1957 and show the robot destroying the mummy. Many other species will suffer the same fate unless we act now!

DONATE NOW!

North American Necrological Research Institute

MIGRATION

While proof of zombie existence earlier than the Stone Age is hard to find, the evidence during that era and afterwards is quite plentiful. Much evidence has been found in archaeological sites connected to early human migration. Aside from the bite-covered skeletal remains of early humans, archaeologists have excavated several burial sites of zombies and their victims along the Bering Strait migration route.

Built as great pits, the burial sites were obviously designed as simple pit traps. The Paleo-Indians must have soon learned that a bitten tribe member quickly became an undead predator. It is believed that only species that reproduced through infectious bites stalked the Paleo-Indians. The still-living infected human was used as bait to lure the undead into the pit. Then the rest of the tribe would bury the unfortunate human victim and zombies, and the shaman would leave fetishes on the site as a warning to others to stay away or perhaps to seal the evil spirits within.

Other evidence of the undead in the Stone Age includes cave drawings, weapons designed to fracture or pierce a human skull, and hundreds of caved-in skulls. Oddly enough, it appears that the peoples of this early era were far better equipped mentally and emotionally to deal with the undead than the civilized humanity of our times. While zombie attacks were frequent, they seldom wiped out tribes. For example, the simple hunter-gatherers of Paleo-America faced death on a daily basis from such dangers as the short-faced bear (*Arctodus* genus), mastodon (*Mammut* genus), or saber-toothed cat (*Smilodon* genus), disease, starvation, weather, or other tribes. The zombie was just one more threat to contend with, and the shamans and medicine men of that time must have guarded vigilantly against the undead. It wasn't until the Neolithic Revolution that humanity let its guard down. Thus, while we commonly believe that our progress as rational beings has been nothing but a pure boon to our species, perhaps we lost something when we lost touch with our savage past.

As humanity took up agriculture, zombie attacks seem to have dropped off. Perhaps the shift in behavior by their prey threw early zombies off or hunter-gatherers were so efficient at destroying undead that by the time agriculture became widespread, there simply weren't enough zombies to be an issue. It is possible that humanity couldn't have progressed until they had stopped the zombie threat.

Above right: The first zombie sieges began approximately with the rise of the first cities. Earlier hunter-gatherer tribes were too scattered and small to attract large numbers of the undead. But cities are stationary targets with large populations, an ideal combination for slow-moving zombies.

Below right: The rise of the first cities was accompanied by the first written accounts of zombie attacks. Uruk, the great capital of Sumerian civilization, produced the Christensen Tablet, a cuneiform poem praising an unknown king for defending it against a horde of "fleshly demons." An English translation is presented at right.

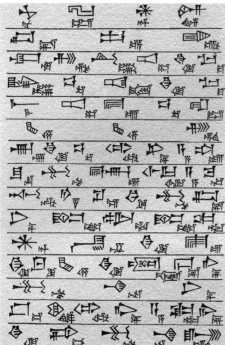

O great king, perfect in your broad wisdom, who preserves Nibru, who saves the city from destruction. Who ordered the gates be closed and kept out the lowly farmers, as they were impure. Who knew that the fleshly demons hid among them, for they were not pious. Who assembled the soldiers of his city and bade them to root out the evil at the gates.

You are the most cherished in all the land! The priests, all-knowing, bless you for restoring peace. For the soldiers did assemble before the gates to face a great host of demons. As befits your calling as lord, you rallied the army and ordered the gates open. Long did they battle the demons, but with spears were their claws kept from rending the flesh.

All but three of the soldiers remained pure, as they were not touched by the demons and thus cursed. O mighty lord, did you order them to be burned, as a sacrifice to appease the spirits that beset your city. May you reign for many years and be greeted by the gods when you ascend to the heavens above!

For whatever reason, zombies simply did not menace early farmers. Unimpeded by the undead, humanity blossomed throughout the world. It wasn't until the dawn of the first civilizations in the Fertile Crescent that their rotting stench fell upon us again.

Uruk marks the start of a pattern of migration that has remained remarkably consistent. Zombies trail after humanity, appearing within the first century of a new civilization or colonization effort. It is true that large gaps appear within the annals of recorded zombie attacks, leading some to believe that zombie migration is more sporadic. However, many times a society will be unaware of the undead until a period of turmoil. The zombie population waxes and wanes inversely to our own. In times of peace and prosperity, the number of undead drops, while in times of war, strife and uncertainty, zombies swell in numbers, overwhelming isolated communities and threatening even large cities. Many lost tribes and civilizations that have disappeared without a trace are thought to be the result of zombie attacks.

Above: Chinese Hopping Corpses are found throughout Southeast Asia, even on remote islands. No doubt they followed shipping routes during their migration.

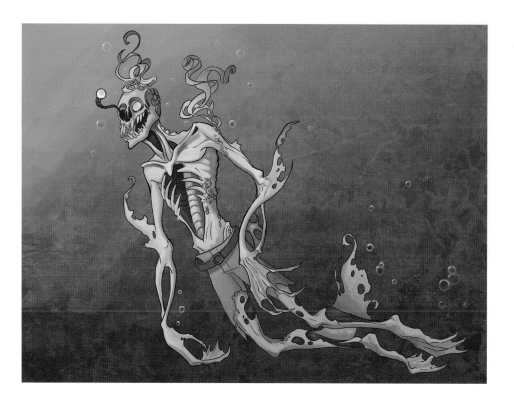

Above: Artist's conception of what an aquatic zombie would look like. Given the size and depth of the world's oceans, it is possible that some undead have evolved to live underwater.

Humans are responsible for much of the zombie's migration. Many undead were inadvertently transported in ships, either by sneaking into the cargo like rats or from infected human sailors and passengers. In some cases, zombies were used directly. The Caribbean was seeded with zombies by pirates in the 18th century through their use of "deadshot": cannon-fired zombies as a weapon of terror. Today's global economy has introduced species to new environs. The Chinese Hopping Corpse can now be found throughout the world as a result of the corpses being shipped out in cargo containers by mistake.

Today, species of zombies can be found anywhere mankind has lingered. It is said that only Antarctica lacks at least one native undead species, and some believe that there is an undiscovered "abominable zombie" out in the frozen wastes. Others believe that an oceanic "mer-zombie" lurks in the deepest ocean depths. Of course, this is only idle speculation. But it is said that where man goes, the undead follow. Perhaps one day we will see zombies trailing us as we colonize the stars, lurching at us in zero gravity.

ADAPTATION

Figure 6-5

Neutralize a talking zombie's mobility by shooting their knees first. Use high-caliber weapons with extreme stopping power to ensure success.

The zombie family shows remarkable variation as each species has adapted to a specific niche in its ecosystem, sometimes even creating the niche in the first place. While many of these variations do not seem to serve any useful purpose, such as the dancing of the Dancing Zombie, many species do adapt to survive. Take the Talking Zombie (*Mortifera immortalis trioxin*) as an example.

Found mostly in urban areas, especially sites with high levels of trioxin pollution, the Talking Zombie preys on especially vulnerable humans: the homeless, petty criminals, drug addicts, prostitutes, and punk rock fans. However, the denizens of skid row are hardened against random violence. A horde of Common Shamblers would be little more than a nuisance to them. In order for a Talking Zombie to kill their prey and devour their brains, they retain their human intelligence and speed while gaining an incredible resistance to injury, resulting in one of the most dangerous zombie species ever to set foot on the earth. Furthermore, Talking Zombies retain the mannerisms of their human hosts, most of whom are punk rock fans. This camouflage prevents early detection by authorities, so they can grow in numbers before

Above and right: Illustrations from the New York City Police Anti-Zombie Tactical Response manual. Several teams of hunters have been trained to hunt down all Talking Zombies within New York. Given the resilience and intelligence of the Talking Zombie, this is a monumentally difficult task. Constant training is essential.

Figure 7-8

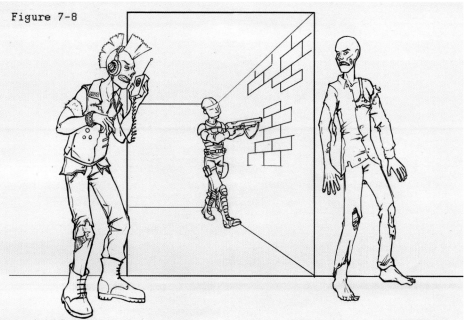

Develop a daily password for communications security.
Talking zombies are smart enough to use captured radios to lure team
members away and ambush them. Beware of calls for more paramedics.

any effort is made to eradicate them. The Talking Zombie has been compared to the rat or cockroach in terms of its resilience. Despite numerous extermination campaigns, the Talking Zombie plagues virtually all major cities. In New York City alone, it is estimated that more than a thousand Talking Zombies lurk in the alleys, derelict buildings, and abandoned subway tunnels at any given time. It is believed that the only reasons Talking Zombies do not overrun the cities are their reliance on trioxin for reproduction and each zombie's personal desire to survive. Each Talking Zombie wishes to survive as long as possible, and infecting too many others too quickly brings it to the attention of the authorities. In many cities, a full-time squad of zombie hunters is deployed year-round to keep their numbers down. The world's premier zombie hunters work in New York City.

The zombie hunters of New York City train all year in order to maintain their edge over the Talking Zombies. Unlike other species, the Talking Zombie is able to adapt as quickly as any human so zombie hunters must constantly revise and change their tactics to stay on top of the food chain. In fact, it seems that the Talking Zombies in the Big Apple talk to

Zombies of the World

each other, keeping tabs on the zombie hunters. Thus, a given tactic may only work once before the Talking Zombies learn how to counter it. For example, zombie hunters initially deployed in an area quietly, without alerting local authorities in order to avoid detection by Talking Zombies. At first this was extremely effective, allowing the hunters to ambush many zombies and destroy them before they could escape. The zombies responded by learning how to exploit the 911 emergency response system. They would flood 911 with calls about armed criminals prowling around, thus flooding the area with police. The ensuing confusion delayed the squad's deployment long enough to give the Talking Zombies time to escape. Now, the hunters coordinate with police and 911 dispatchers when they deploy.

The Talking Zombie's case is hardly the only example of zombie adaptation, but it highlights the versatility of the undead when it comes to surviving in a hostile environment. Most species of zombie produce an instinctive revulsion in humans and other animals, provoking a fight-or-flight response. Yet despite our best efforts to wipe them off the face of the earth, they stubbornly refuse to fade away into the night. Few other species can survive facing such determined opposition. We must give the zombie credit for its survival. In truth, this is yet another reason why zombie research is such an important undertaking. Its resilience could be the key to our survival.

The evolution of the zombie is one of the primary topics of research in the field. By understanding how and why certain species evolve as they do, we might be able to ascertain the true nature of the *Omega Anima* or at least find a way to harvest its bounty. Currently, NANRI is exploring several avenues towards understanding zombie adaptation, each using the perspective of a different academic discipline. Dr. Linda Hasting has pioneered a sign language program to teach Egyptian Mummies how to communicate with the living. A team led by Dr. Robert Bava is pursuing clean energy generation through Shambler-powered stationary bicycles. Finally, NANRI has created a unique undead sanctuary, where researchers protect various endangered species for future preservation efforts.

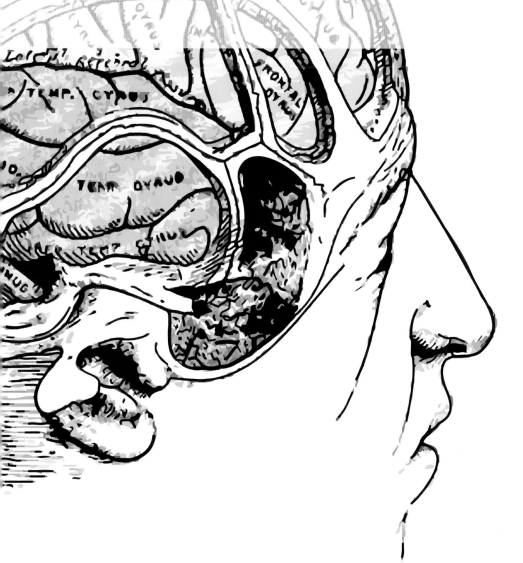

ZOMBIE SPECIES

How to read this section

This guide covers the 20 most prominent species of zombies. Each description is written in the following format.

Conservation Status: Each species of zombie is assigned a conservation status to indicate its probability of becoming extinct, given current trends. Five statuses are recognized.

1. Extinct – No active specimens have been found for 50 years, and no more are believed to exist in the wild. Depending on how the species reproduces, more may arise, but this is unlikely.

2. Must Exterminate – A species inimical to human life that must be destroyed in order to prevent our species from becoming extinct.

3. Critically Endangered – The population of the species is extremely small or current environmental trends will render its ability to survive in the wild impossible within 20 years.

4. Vulnerable – The species is likely to become endangered within 20 years unless current survival and reproduction trends change.

5. Least Concern – The population of the species is viable and has a very low risk of becoming extinct.

Name: The common name and scientific name are given. Note that many species have common names that may seem misleading. For example, the New England Ghoul is found in Europe and North America, despite its name.

Description: The physical characteristics of the species are detailed. If a species has unusual traits, such as the Nukekubi's ability to levitate, then it will be mentioned in this section. Individuals within a species can vary widely in their appearance, especially in species such as the Preta.

Habits and Habitat: The typical behavior of the species is explained with a focus on how it acquires prey and survives in its habitat. Unusual or unique behavioral highlights are emphasized, such as the Draugr's preference for attacking armed warriors. The habitat is the species' preferred environment, as it is possible to find a specimen outside of its natural habitat.

Reproduction: Zombies have extremely varied means of reproduction. Many simply transform living humans by infecting them with a virus. Other species spontaneously arise from human corpses that fit certain criteria, such as the Revenant or Preta. Some are created artificially. In many cases we do not know how the species is created.

Range: Where the species is commonly encountered.

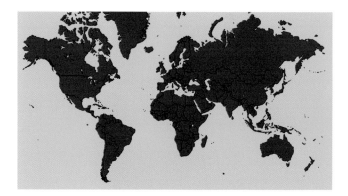

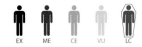

COMMON GRAY SHAMBLER
Mortifera immortalis romeroi

Conservation Status: Least Concern

Description: The Shambler appears as an animated human corpse, walking in a shuffling manner. It is slow and dim-witted, only able to use basic tools and unable to open doors or climb ladders. Their bodies decay slower than a normal corpse and decay appears to stop entirely before the Shambler falls apart. While they are functionally immortal, the Shambler does not heal and as a result most Shamblers bear at least one grotesque injury.

Habits and Habitat: Shamblers are instinctive herd animals, commonly gathering in large groups. The proper name for such a group is a horde. They are wanderers, attracted by loud noises, bright lights, or other intense visual or auditory stimuli. They exclusively prey on living humans and recently deceased human corpses, seeking to eat as much flesh as possible. Once a Shambler has locked on a target, it will stalk them until destroyed or a more viable prey presents itself.

Despite many attempts to exterminate them by various governments, they shamble on, the ultimate survivors. Shamblers are one of the few species that may be legally hunted in the United States in limited numbers. Its apparent inability to pose a threat to a human may be an evolutionary strategy to lull its victims into a state of complacency.

Shamblers are found throughout the world. Sporadic flare-ups of Shamblers appear in urban and suburban areas every 15 to 30 years, requiring a managed culling of the horde. Shamblers can also be found in remote wilderness regions, separated from their hordes and unnoticed by humanity. It is believed that many Shambler hordes are started by hikers or hunters who found an isolated zombie, became infected, and returned to civilization.

It should be noted that despite urban legends to the contrary, Shamblers do not wander the bottom of the world's oceans. Despite their resilience, the pressure destroys them as surely as it would a normal human.

Reproduction: As a parasitic species, the Shambler infects humans through physical contact. They prefer to bite and claw their victims. This is how most, but not all, infections happen. It is also possible to become infected by breathing air that carries residual Shambler viscera. Thus, while a chainsaw, automatic shotgun, or explosive might be a tempting weapon to use against a Shambler, keep in mind that the fine red mist of the remains of a Shambler is just as deadly as the creature itself.

Range: Global range, but most commonly found in urban and suburban sprawl of First World countries.

Common Gray Shambler

Mortifera immortalis romeroi

The age of a Shambler can be determined by the degree of decay and the pallor of its skin.

Shamblers hold on to their prey with amazing tenacity. Severing the arm or hand is easier than trying to break a Shambler's grip.

CHINESE HOPPING CORPSE
Mortifera immortalis jiang-shi

Conservation Status: Least Concern

Description: An animated Chinese human corpse with a blue/gray skin coloration, almost always dressed in Qing Dynasty-era clothing. Many Hopping Corpses have extremely long fingernails that are razor sharp and quite dangerous. Extremely long tongues are another common feature. Their name comes from their peculiar habit of hopping instead of walking, shuffling, shambling, or staggering. A normal Hopping Corpse hops with arms outstretched in a stiff manner.

Habits and Habitat: The Chinese Hopping Corpse is a solitary predator by nature, although small groups have been found. They prefer to waylay isolated travelers and rip them apart with their claws and teeth, although anyone who is alone is a potential target. Equipped with a highly attuned sense of hearing, the Hopping Corpse can track a target that makes any sound whatsoever. Anecdotal evidence indicates that even breathing makes enough noise for this species to track.

Their primary habitats are isolated roads, abandoned Taoist temples and homes that have bad feng shui. With the rise of manufacturing for export, the Hopping Corpse has migrated to the factory towns of China. Striking in poorly guarded worker dormitories or even in the factories themselves, the Hopping Corpse has become a major problem that has been exported to the rest of the world.

At first believed to be an urban legend, several reports have confirmed that Hopping Corpses have been found throughout the world, transported by Chinese shipping containers and crates. At this point we don't know how the undead found their way into containers, but despite some efforts to stop their spread, they have

infested many coastal cities and are working their way inland.

Formerly found only in Asia, this species has expanded its range to encompass most of the globe by hitching rides with freight exported from China. While some confuse them with the Common Gray Shambler, this species has a vastly different physiology. Most importantly, it is not especially vulnerable to head injuries or blunt force trauma.

Reproduction: The exact mechanism of how a dead human becomes a Hopping Corpse is still unknown. For all intents and purposes, certain people of Chinese descent simply arise as a Hopping Corpse after death. The Hopping Corpse does not infect humans with their bites or claws. The only mystery greater than why some people arise as Hopping Corpses is how all of them are able to obtain Qing Dynasty-era clothing.

Range: Until the last 20 years, the Hopping Corpse was restricted to mainland China. Today, the species is active in many major coastal cities around the world that import goods from Chinese factories. Furthermore, they are moving inland, with several sightings in landlocked cities such as Mexico City and Las Vegas.

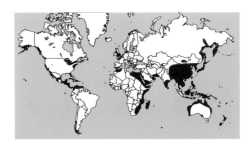

CHINESE HOPPING CORPSE
Mortifera immortalis jiang-shi

The fingernails are much stronger than normal. Their tensile strength is roughly twice that of human bone. The tips are razor sharp.

Only an estimated 65 percent of Hopping Corpses have elongated tongues. Scientists still aren't sure what purpose the tongue serves.

EGYPTIAN MUMMY
Mortifera mumia aegyptus

EX   ME   CE   VU   LC

Conservation Status: Critically Endangered

Description: A completely desiccated corpse, wrapped in strips of linen cloth. The flesh is blackened from thousands of years in a dry desert environment. At first believed to be Common Shamblers that underwent the mummification process, we now realize this is a separate species. After all, a Shambler dies if its brain is destroyed. The mummification ritual removes the brain through the nose with an iron hook. The Egyptian Mummy is still poorly understood by scientists, who are only now beginning to learn its symbiotic relationship with the leaves of the tanna plant.

Habits and Habitat: This species seems to be motivated by an aggressive sense of territoriality. It jealously guards its tomb from potential thieves and vandals, killing them by strangulation. The rest of its time is spent in a deep torpor, dreaming of ages past. Mummies are an intelligent species, able to learn sign language if properly taught. However, they have a very anti-social outlook which makes communication difficult. Their intelligence despite the lack of a brain is a total mystery to scientists.

Mummies are still found in the deserts of Egypt, especially in the Valley of the Kings. When they were designated an endangered species, the Egyptian government went to great lengths to keep poachers from destroying the few active mummies. A few tombs have become popular tourist attractions, where visitors hope to see a wild mummy leave its tomb to scare off potential thieves.

Strangely, the only other known population is in London. At least five mummies roam the sewers and archives near the British Museum. It is believed that they were brought into the city during the 19th century and have hidden in the massive archives and tunnels around the museum. The mummies seem to be quite benign to most museum staff, although they are suspected of killing a few vagrants and thieves over the years. Still, as a protected species, they are allowed to roam free until a way to return them to Egypt can be determined.

Reproduction: Egyptian Mummies are an artificial species in a sense, as humans play a part in their creation. All of them were made in ancient Egypt through religious funerary practices that incorporated the leaves of the tanna plant, although how the leaves were used is still unknown. This rare plant is the difference between an inert corpse and an active mummy. We do not know if the ancient Egyptians intended to animate the corpses or if the mummy is an accidental by-product of the ritual. Despite several attempts to reproduce the mummification process, no one has been able to create a modern Egyptian Mummy.

Range: Africa and London. Most prevalent adjacent to ruins of the Third Dynasty. Occasionally, inexplicably found in remote deserts. These xeric habitats may have at one time been lush oases occupied by slave traders and banished royalty. Their perishable shelters disappeared eons ago, but the homeless, solitary zombified mummies persist in these desolate places, observed only by smugglers and lost National Geographic Society photographers.

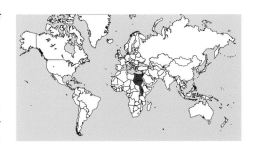

Egyptian Mummy
Mortifera mumia aegyptus

Despite their high intelligence, Egyptian Mummies are unable to speak except for a low, guttural moan. This inability to communicate may explain their anger.

The bones of this species are brittle and easily broken. Should you encounter one, taking a knee out with a quick kick is a good tactic.

AZTEC MUMMY

Mortifera mumia mictlantecuhtli

EX ME CE VU LC

Conservation Status: Extinct

Description: A withered mummified corpse, typically dressed in the clothing of one of the Mesoamerican cultures. Despite what the name implies, Mayan and Incan Mummies have also been discovered in a few cases, but the species was named by conquistadors during the conquest of the Aztec civilization. Sadly, the species is believed to be extinct, but some hold out hope that a few Aztec Mummies still exist.

Habits and Habitat: Little is known of the habits of the Aztec Mummy. The codices of the Aztec people were mostly destroyed by Spanish missionaries and the few Western writers who witnessed an Aztec Mummy did not record much useful information about them. What little information remains suggests that the mummy was relatively peaceful, although that may be due to the steady diet of human sacrificial victims given to the mummies by the Aztec priests.

When the conquistadors arrived, they brought robots, an invasive vermin that preyed upon the Aztec Mummy and drove them to extinction. While many people do not understand why robots suddenly appeared in Europe in the 16th century and have plagued us ever since, there is strong evidence to indicate that some type of time travel is responsible for their introduction. The common robot is a canny scavenger, able to survive on nearly any kind of fuel, but it apparently favored the desiccated corpses of Aztec Mummies, which apparently burned quite well. While the topic of time-displaced robots is a fascinating one, it is beyond the scope of this book. If you wish to learn more about the topic, pick up a copy of *Robots in History* by Scott Daniels or any of the many other books on the subject.

The last known sighting of an Aztec Mummy occurred in 1957, when a filmmaker caught a battle between the mummy and a robot. Tragically, the mummy lost the battle.

Unconfirmed sightings of Aztec Mummies have been reported for hundreds of years, mostly in the remote parts of north and central Mexico. In the last decade, these reports have skyrocketed, leading to wild stories about a masked Aztec Mummy that protects the weak and wrestles villains into submission. This Aztec Luchador is no doubt a folktale.

Reproduction: Unknown. It is theorized that, like the Egyptian Mummy, creation of a mummy involved Aztec funerary rituals that are now lost to the sands of time.

Range: Formerly Central America.

Aztec Mummy

Mortifera mumia mictlantecuhtli

Aztec Mummies often wore gold jewelry, which may explain why the Spanish conquistadors were so eager to destroy them.

REVENANT
Mortifera reverto voorheesi

Conservation Status: Critically Endangered

Description: A Revenant is a zombie that spontaneously arises from a human unjustly killed, typically within 24 hours after death. The Revenant is motivated by an intense desire for revenge against anyone it blames for its death. They appear much as they did in life except for a grayish pallor, as the Revenant hardly decays at all. They are noticeably stronger than they were in life. Revenants have ripped car doors off their hinges and bent steel bars when in pursuit of their chosen prey.

Habits and Habitat: The typical Revenant is murdered by several unrepentant killers who are unpunished by society. The Revenant stalks each killer in turn to murder them in gruesome and sadistic ways. Once all of its targets are dead, many Revenants simply die, often returning to their original grave sites. However, other Revenants become territorial killers that attack any who wander too close to their grave, especially those who remind them of their original killers.

Revenants are highly intelligent for zombies, able to use tools and formulate long-term plans. Despite this, they are uncommunicative. Most are mute, and the few that do speak only do so to threaten or terrify their victims. It is interesting to note that the Revenant's reasoning when it comes to picking its victims is highly variable. In fact, many Revenants go after people only tangentially connected to their death.

For example, consider the case of Alfred Donaldson, a long-term smoker who died of lung cancer in 1993 after his insurance provider stopped paying for treatment. Mr. Donaldson arose only minutes after his death and proceeded to kill his doctor, the entire hospital billing department, three security guards, and a janitor. He then traveled over 600 miles to the headquarters of his insurance company and butchered more than thirty executives before being destroyed by a SWAT team. Detectives recovered maps and other evidence indicating that the Revenant planned to attack the tobacco company that manufactured his favorite brand of cigarette. As a precaution, the police used white phosphorus grenades to incinerate his corpse on the spot in order to prevent another attack.

Reproduction: What triggers the creation of a Revenant is poorly understood. Many theories abound in the field, but all available evidence seems to indicate that the human host and the cause of death are the most important factors. Case studies of Revenants show that many Revenant hosts were extremely sensitive to perceived injustices and/or had anger issues. Prior to his (un)death, Alfred Donaldson made several vitriolic statements against his doctor and the insurance company, blaming them for his poor treatment and health. His death was extremely prolonged and painful by all accounts. However, such anecdotal evidence has failed to yield a workable theory of Revenant creation. Revenants are an endangered species, as fewer than a thousand have been found in the last 75 years.

Range: Global. They have been found on every continent, even Antarctica in one tragic case. A Revenant traveled to Antarctica to kill one particular victim. It fled the continent after the murder.

REVENANT
Mortifera reverto voorheesi

Revenants exhibit great resilience, even when compared to other zombies. Their flesh is significantly denser than human flesh, allowing them to shrug off injuries that would fell other undead.

Headshots do not necessarily kill Revenants. Anything short of decapitation or complete destruction of the body is unlikely to stop one.

Weapons are commonly employed by Revenants. While they are quite strong, they tend to prefer bladed weapons. In recent years, they have been reported to use firearms.

EX   ME   CE   VU   LC

HAITIAN ZOMBIE
Mortifera vodou samedi

Conservation Status: Vulnerable

Description: A malnourished human in a deep trance state. Haitian Zombies are much closer to humans than any other zombie species as they breathe and bleed like a normal human. However, the process that transforms a human into a Haitian Zombie creates physiological changes in the brain and body. Haitian Zombies have the same endless endurance of the other species, an endurance that can only come from the *Omega Anima*. They also have the GHUL genetic markers that signify their transformation into a new species. However, unlike any other known species of zombie, Haitian Zombies can be made human again through a prolonged therapeutic process.

Habits and Habitats: Haitian Zombies are made by *bokors* (witch doctors) in a secretive ritual that incorporates neurotoxins and several drops of blood from a Gray Shambler. They are typically used as manual laborers and guards by their creators. Considered the first true artificial species of undead, the Haitian Zombie is notoriously prone to rebel against its master, especially a cruel and oppressive one. Once the zombie can escape or kill its master, it will wander aimlessly, sometimes trying to reunite with friends and family. Tragically, the zombie is usually slain quickly, either by fearful villagers or by grieving family members.

Unique among the zombies of the world, a Haitian Zombie can be converted back into a human. Pioneered by a team of therapists at the Université d'Etat d'Haiti in 1986, humanization therapy is a long process of gradual reintegration that takes months or even years to finish. The zombie is first forced to sleep, then eat and drink like a normal human until the body begins to rejuvenate itself.

The zombie gains intelligence and memories of its past life and finally is reintroduced into society while a counselor assists the new human with all parts of their life. The GHUL genetic markers remain in the new human's DNA, but they become inert – junk chromosomes that do not affect the person.

Reproduction: Haitian Zombies can only be created through a specific ritual that is known by a few witch doctors in Haiti.

Range: Haiti and parts of Louisiana. It is believed several ingredients used in the creation ritual are unique to Haiti, so it is thought that *bokors* must remain nearby to acquire them. All ingredients are gathered and processed by the *bokor* personally to ensure they are prepared correctly. In Louisiana, they are rarely found farther than 75 kilometers north of New Orleans. Not found in estuarial environments south of New Orleans. In Cajun folklore, this species is said to attack cottonmouth water moccasins whose venomous bite apparently produces a mild euphoric effect for them. After holding the reptiles close to their face and being envenomated, the *Mortifera vodou samedi* performs a cycle of hopping and vocalizations that local fishermen interpret as dancing. The cottonmouth (*Agkistrodon piscivorus*) avoids brackish water, so this may explain this zombie's preference for freshwater swamp habitat.

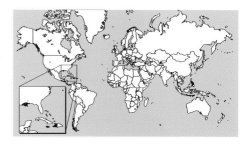

HAITIAN ZOMBIE

Mortifera vodou samedi

Haitian Zombies frequently recall memories of their previous human life, more than any other species. Friends and family are safe from rampaging Haitian Zombies.

GHOUL
Mortifera immortalis persis

Conservation Status: Vulnerable

Description: A rail-thin animated human corpse with talon-like fingernails, often more than four inches in length. Ghouls are noted for their hideous stench and poor dress. They typically wear whatever rags they find that best camouflage them. Ghouls are notorious gluttons, unable to control themselves when presented with carrion, human or animal.

Arabian poets first wrote of Ghouls as mythical demons, but by the Middle Ages, scholars described them in more concrete terms, as diseased cannibals who dwelt in cemeteries and deserts. It wasn't until the 19th century that the existence of the Ghoul was reported in the West. A British naturalist, Sir Randolph Carter, barely survived an attack by a Ghoul in the deserts of Iraq and managed to decapitate it with a shovel. Sir Randolph examined the corpse and realized he had discovered a new species of the undead.

Habits and Habitat: Originating in the Middle East, Ghouls are canny opportunists that will kill the living or feast on the dead with equal fervor. They prefer to ambush isolated victims and devour their entire corpse over a period of days. If a victim manages to survive the initial ambush, the Ghoul will usually flee, as it is a cowardly creature.

Since the rise of urbanization and globalization in the Middle East, Ghouls have spread to the squalor of the numerous ghettoes and shantytowns scattered throughout the region. Numerous reports have surfaced of Ghoul attacks, even in broad daylight. They are considered a vermin species to be shot on sight.

Ghouls rarely gather in groups larger than a dozen, but when they do gather, they become effective pack hunters. They are quick to utilize advanced tactics, such as flanking and ambushing their prey, while some reports indicate they are capable of great patience, stalking a chosen target for hours or even days before striking. It is thought the Ghoul adapted due to the relative scarcity of prey in its favored desert environs. Ghouls that find themselves in an urban environment are extremely dangerous, as their tactics work well in the confined quarters of a city.

Reproduction: Ghouls reproduce in a similar manner to Gray Shamblers: through infection transmitted by physical contact with a Ghoul. A victim bitten or clawed by a Ghoul invariably transforms into one if they aren't eaten. Unlike the Shambler, this process can take weeks or months to complete. Fortunately, an infected victim cannot spread the disease until the transformation is complete.

Range: Once confined only to the Middle East, the Ghoul has spread to neighboring regions in Africa, Asia and Europe. A few have even been found in Brazil and the United States, transported by ships. Experts believe it is only a matter of time before Ghouls become a major urban problem in port cities around the world.

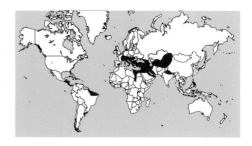

GHOUL
Mortifera immortalis persis

Middle Eastern folklore states that traditional weapons are more effective than firearms in dispatching Ghouls. There is no scientific evidence to support this belief.

Ghouls seem to be compelled to dress in medieval Arabic attire even if not of Middle Eastern descent. It is not known how they are able to find such clothing so consistently.

DRAUGR
Mortifera immortalis norse

EX   ME   CE   VU   LC

Conservation Status: Critically Endangered

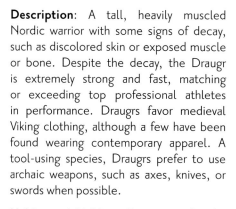

Description: A tall, heavily muscled Nordic warrior with some signs of decay, such as discolored skin or exposed muscle or bone. Despite the decay, the Draugr is extremely strong and fast, matching or exceeding top professional athletes in performance. Draugrs favor medieval Viking clothing, although a few have been found wearing contemporary apparel. A tool-using species, Draugrs prefer to use archaic weapons, such as axes, knives, or swords when possible.

Habits and Habitat: Draugrs prefer the deep wilderness far from civilization. A species motivated by psychological needs rather than basic sustenance, Draugrs are driven to seek out and defeat worthy opponents in battle, typically to the death. The exact modus operandi is unique to the individual Draugr. Some prefer to fight a single opponent in a ritualized duel, usually with a specific weapon, while others will target groups of humans and use stealth and cunning to ambush and kill as many as possible. They typically only target healthy adult males or large predatory animals as opponents, but they have attacked women bearing arms.

Feared throughout Europe for centuries, the Draugr was thought to be invincible before the invention of gunpowder. The undead warriors are all but immune to hand-to-hand combat. It takes artillery or powerful explosives to reliably stop a berserk Draugr. Ever since the first successful Draugr hunt in the 14th century, it was fashionable for the aristocracy to hunt these majestic undead warriors for sport. Once numbering in the thousands, there are only a few dozen Draugrs known to exist. Fortunately, activists are working to protect the remaining Draugrs from poachers and malicious hunters.

Reproduction: Similar to the Revenant, Draugrs spontaneously arise, although the Draugr is far more specific. It is believed that warriors or soldiers of Norse ancestry who die in their prime without being able to die in combat are the most likely candidates to become a Draugr. However, unlike the Revenant, we are not certain why some soldiers rise as Draugrs and others do not. What is certain is that the Draugr does not rise as much as it used to; the youngest known Draugr is a Finnish ski-trooper who died in World War II fighting the Nazis.

Range: Found almost solely in Europe, mostly in Scandinavia, but also as far south as northern Italy. A subpopulation in the Italian Alps is slightly smaller than the Scandinavian population. As there are slight physiological and behavioral differences, some authorities believe the Italian population should be considered taxonomically distinct. A small disjunct population was introduced to Drake Island, off the coast of Florida.

DRAUGR
Mortifera immortalis norse

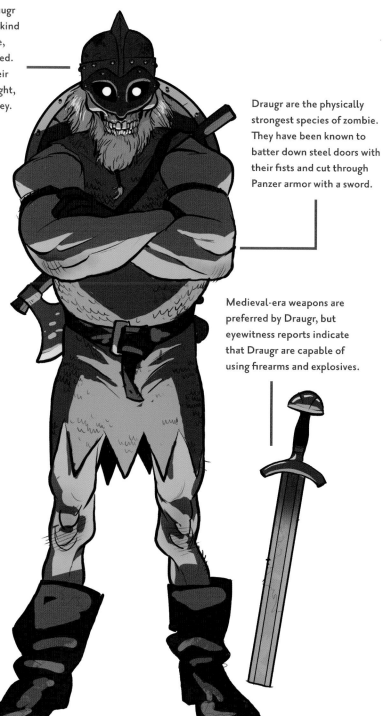

The eyes of the Draugr appear to exhibit a kind of bioluminescence, glowing yellow or red. While this gives their location away at night, it unnerves most prey.

Draugr are the physically strongest species of zombie. They have been known to batter down steel doors with their fists and cut through Panzer armor with a sword.

Medieval-era weapons are preferred by Draugr, but eyewitness reports indicate that Draugr are capable of using firearms and explosives.

NUKEKUBI
Mortifera immortalis kwaidan

Conservation Status: Vulnerable

Description: A levitating human head, typically decayed. The Nukekubi is able to propel itself through unknown means approximately 5 to 6 feet off the ground. Found throughout Asia under a variety of names, such as *aswang* and *manananggal*, the Nukekubi was first studied by Western scientists in Japan in 1904.

Perhaps the most exotic species of zombie known to man due to their uncanny ability to levitate, they were classified as a separate family until DNA testing found the GHUL markers and confirmed their inclusion in the *Mortifera* family. In folklore, the Nukekubi are said to have bodies they attach to during the day, but this is not true. Their bodies disintegrate soon after the transformation into the undead. Their top speed is unknown, but it is believed to be in the 10- to 20-miles-per-hour range.

Habits and Habitat: The Nukekubi is a cruel predator. It does eat the flesh of the living, but due to its small size, it can only eat a few mouthfuls. Like a cat, it enjoys toying with its victims by terrorizing them with prolonged chases and scaring them with horrifying screams when they least expect it. Sometimes it even spares a particularly emotive victim, just so it can terrify them another night. A pack hunter, they gather in groups of six to twelve.

The Nukekubi is semi-nomadic, lingering in a given area for a few weeks or months before moving on. They stay long enough to claim a few victims and leave before a search party can find and dispatch them. Of course, finding a Nukekubi is harder than it seems. They can be completely silent and their ability to levitate allows them to hide nearly anywhere.

Scientists in Japan have implemented a GPS tag tracking program to monitor the Nukekubi. It has met with some controversy as many people simply wish to exterminate them, citing the danger they pose to humans.

Reproduction: Nukekubi reproduce through an airborne infection. Victims grow weaker over a period of 12 hours after initial infection until they die, at which point the body rapidly decays while the head undergoes a metamorphosis into a Nukekubi. Nukekubi are carriers of the disease, as they spread the disease wherever they fly. Fortunately, as this is a bacterial disease, antibiotics can be used to treat the infection. However, few victims receive treatment in time, as the Nukekubi prefer to dwell in rural areas, where medical treatment is hard to come by.

Range: The Nukekubi are found throughout Asia in rural and wild regions. They have not successfully adapted to urbanization, but as humanity encroaches on their territory, this may change.

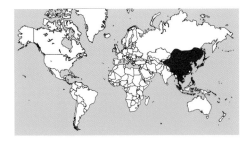

NUKEKUBI

Mortifera immortalis kwaidan

The ability to fly and levitate in place is one of the greatest mysteries of this species. Physicists are still unable to explain how they are able to defy gravity in this manner.

The teeth of the Nukekubi transform into long fangs within days of creation. They are so long they actually interfere with biting, but their appearance certainly terrifies its prey.

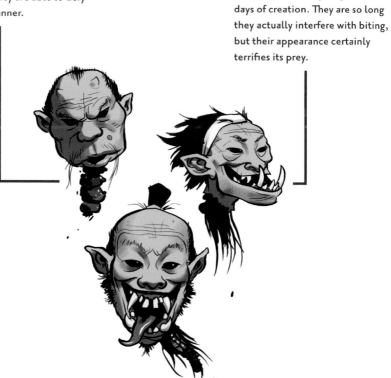

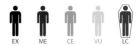

REANIMATED ZOMBIE
Mortifera facticius westi

Conservation Status: Least Concern

Description: An animated human corpse, typically dressed in a hospital gown, tagged or tattooed in a manner consistent with lab animals. They are usually well preserved and may even be mistaken for a living human, at least initially. They move in a slow and awkward manner. The progenitor serum, the substance used to create the Reanimated Zombie, is a bright fluorescent green and many Reanimated Zombies seep small amounts of the serum, a trait that can help a keen observer distinguish one from a Gray Shambler.

Habits and Habitat: Created in 1921 through the progenitor serum developed by Dr. Herbert West, the Reanimated Zombie has become the lab animal of choice for medical labs throughout the world for decades until various treaties made the practice illegal. Many are still used by unethical researchers and little is being done to enforce existing laws and treaties.

Reanimated Zombies are interesting because while they are as murderous as the Gray Shambler, they are seldom as hungry. A Reanimated Zombie prefers to strangle or beat its victims to death and they seldom consume any of their victims' flesh.

As an artificial species, the Reanimated Zombie has no natural habitat. They are typically only found in lab environments, as researchers take extraordinary precautions to avoid any mishap. Still, some have escaped, and when given a chance, they prefer urban environments, particularly warehouses, abandoned buildings, and other isolated areas.

Reproduction: Only the progenitor serum can create a Reanimated Zombie. The Reanimated Zombie cannot infect a human although residual exposure to the serum from a bite may be enough to trigger the transformation. Even environmental exposure from nearby spills of the serum can create a Reanimated Zombie.

The serum is a highly controlled substance, available only to a few authorized institutions trusted to use it in a responsible manner, but it was an unregulated chemical until 1955. As a consequence, many experimented with the serum and dumped it wherever they could when they finished their research. Old dump sites are still being discovered. Tragically, no one knows how much of the serum was dumped around the world or what the long-term consequences will be.

Range: Global. Reanimated Zombies can appear anywhere as a result of the progenitor serum's release into the environment.

REANIMATED ZOMBIE

Mortifera facticius westi

Most Reanimated Zombies show signs of their origin – tags or identification cards that name the lab responsible for their creation.

While they are always restrained in the laboratories in which they are kept, Reanimated Zombies are adept escape artists. It is believed that more than 30 percent of all Reanimated Zombies created eventually manage to escape.

EX ME CE VU LC

Conservation Status: Vulnerable

ITALIAN ZOMBIE
Mortifera immortalis fulci

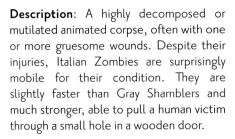

Description: A highly decomposed or mutilated animated corpse, often with one or more gruesome wounds. Despite their injuries, Italian Zombies are surprisingly mobile for their condition. They are slightly faster than Gray Shamblers and much stronger, able to pull a human victim through a small hole in a wooden door.

Habits and Habitat: A particularly nasty species, the Italian Zombie is noted for its gory feeding habits. It makes a point of dismembering and mutilating its victims beyond the point of recognition. This may seem to be unnecessarily sadistic, but it paralyzes nearby prey with terror, thus making them easy targets for the zombie. It also cuts down on the number of zombies created during an attack, thus reducing the competition for prey.

Such divergence from the norm suggests that natural selection has resulted in seemingly counter-intuitive tactics. Perhaps by naturally limiting their numbers, the Italian Zombie avoids detection longer and thus is able to survive longer than the Gray Shambler. Their most divergent trait though is their amphibious nature.

Italian Zombies are at home in the water, either walking along the bottom or swimming in a basic dogpaddle. This was confirmed when a noted Italian oceanographer filmed a battle between an Italian Zombie and a shark. This infamous encounter has been shown in countless documentaries about the zombie and has fed anti-zombie hysteria and misinformation ever since.

A wave of Italian Zombie attacks in the 1970s and early 1980s resulted in a mass hunt for them throughout Europe. In one famous case in 1971, a castle in Spain was found to hold dozens of Italian Zombies dating back to the Middle Ages. The zombies were former Knights Templar, still clad in armor. When archeologists unwittingly released them, they spread throughout Europe.

Thousands were destroyed, leading some to believe that they were driven to extinction. However, they have recovered since then. A few survived by hiding underwater or in remote tombs.

Reproduction: The Italian Zombie spreads an airborne disease that infects all humans who come into close contact with it. Once the human dies, regardless of cause, it will transform into an Italian Zombie within minutes.

Range: Primarily found in southern Europe, but specimens have been found in North America and Asia. Due to its amphibious nature, the Italian Zombie is not hindered by any but the deepest oceans and has shown up in remote locales like Easter Island.

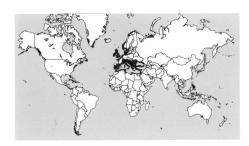

ITALIAN ZOMBIE
Mortifera immortalis fulci

Injuries to the sensory organs do not
impair the senses of the Italian Zombie.

ENGLISH FOAMING ZOMBIE
Mortifera rabies londinium

Conservation Status: Must Exterminate

Description: A human in the throes of a psychotic rage, typically foaming at the mouth and covered in blood. A highly manic species, the English Foaming Zombie is noted for its speed and ferocity. Many victims are caught off guard by the Foaming Zombie's agility due to its deceptive idle state. When a Foaming Zombie is not hunting, it has a tendency to go into a trance-like state, where it moves slowly. When it detects a victim, it springs into action, attacking them with brute force. This species does not feed on its victims, only killing them before moving on.

Habits and Habitat: At first believed to be normal humans merely suffering from a variant of rabies, the 2002 London outbreak convinced researchers that a new species of zombie had been discovered when genetic testing revealed the presence of the GHUL genetic markers.

Strangely, the English Foaming Zombie is just as vulnerable as a normal human. In fact, it is susceptible to starvation, a unique weakness among all species of the undead. This has led many to question its status as a real zombie species. A vocal minority of scientists has protested the decision to list the English Foaming Zombie as a recognized species of the undead. They insist that the English Foaming Zombies be reclassified as infected humans. They believe that a cure capable of reversing the transformation will be found. So far, little progress has been made on a cure.

Many scientists believe the Foaming Zombie is genetically flawed, unable to properly draw sustenance from the *Omega Anima* and thus is a doomed species. While it can transform many humans quickly, the Foaming Zombie is doomed to die within a few weeks of its creation from starvation. Fortunately, this flaw prevents them from becoming a major threat to humanity. Interestingly, other zombie species may also help protect us from outbreaks.

It is common knowledge that zombies generally do not attack one another. While they may fight over territory or a human corpse, the undead do not view each other as food. However, English Foaming Zombies are generally viewed as prey by other zombie species. In several reported cases, other urban zombie species, such as the Talking Zombie, have preyed upon English Foaming Zombies. In fact, other zombies seem to prefer them over normal humans. Perhaps this form of predation can be used to our benefit.

Reproduction: An incredibly virulent species, as a single drop of blood can infect a human, with a 99.7 percent transformation rate. Fortunately, due to the short life span of the Foaming Zombie and quick response by anti-zombie security agencies, the English Foaming Zombie does not pose an existential threat to the human species.

Range: First found in London, England, but can be found throughout Europe. Given current trends, it will have a global range within 10 years.

ENGLISH FOAMING ZOMBIE
Mortifera rabies londinium

All bodily fluids of this species are capable of infecting a human.

It should be noted that being scratched by an English Foaming Zombie does not infect a human, unless the zombie's blood falls on the scratch.

The speed of this species is its most dangerous trait. Even specimens that were in poor shape in their human life can run with great speed and endurance.

NEW ENGLAND GHOUL
Mortifera immortalis pickmani

Conservation Status: Vulnerable

Description: A roughly bipedal humanoid with vaguely canine legs and cloven hooves. Skin tone is usually grayish-blue, although individual ghouls vary widely. The mouth is heavily deformed, taking on a canine appearance, with powerful jaws and a muzzle instead of a mouth.

New England Ghouls are unique in nature for one trait: they are bipedal ungulates. Scientists still do not understand the evolutionary advantage for this trait. Extensive studies have been conducted on their gait and how it benefits the species.

Habits and Habitat: The inspiration behind the infamous artwork of its discoverer, Richard Pickman, this species is known for its nocturnal carrion feeding habits and is a common sight in poorly guarded graveyards. It will not attack a living creature unless provoked or threatened. The New England Ghoul prefers to consume human corpses although it does not gain sustenance from eating. They appear to suffer a complete obsession with consuming dead human flesh. They will not eat a live human.

An intelligent species, the New England Ghoul is capable of speech and complex thought. Recent studies hypothesize it may be able to learn what a human knew by consuming their cerebrum, although this has not been confirmed.

In 1973, a New England Ghoul was found in the walls of a castle in southern France. The creature had been immured for centuries, yet it was still active. Unfortunately, it was destroyed by superstitious villagers before it could be questioned. It is hoped one day that New England Ghouls will come forward to share their unique perspective on history. As an immortal species, individual ghouls may have lived through many of the great events that shaped our world.

Reproduction: It is believed that humans become New England Ghouls through ritualistic cannibalism. The transformation is an extremely prolonged process, and it is believed that Ghouls purposefully seek out depraved humans in order to lure them into a path of cannibalism. Eventually, a cannibal undergoes a form of metamorphosis into a New England Ghoul. Regions that suffer from extreme famine often create minor populations of New England Ghouls as desperate humans turn to cannibalism to survive. These ghouls are usually slain upon discovery. Only the ghouls that learn how to hide their feeding habits survive more than a few months.

Range: Most established in the oldest cities of North America, especially the Yankee strongholds. There is a sparse disjunct population in the southwestern United States and northern Mexico. Encountered throughout Europe in older graveyards and cemeteries. A colony of several dozen is believed to live in the Paris Catacombs.

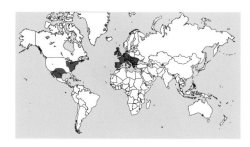

NEW ENGLAND GHOUL
Mortifera immortalis pickmani

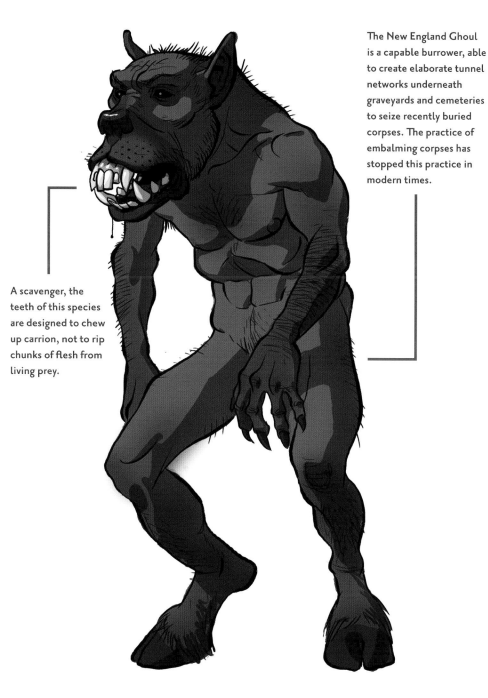

The New England Ghoul is a capable burrower, able to create elaborate tunnel networks underneath graveyards and cemeteries to seize recently buried corpses. The practice of embalming corpses has stopped this practice in modern times.

A scavenger, the teeth of this species are designed to chew up carrion, not to rip chunks of flesh from living prey.

TALKING ZOMBIE
Mortifera immortalis trioxin

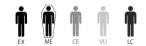

EX   ME   CE   VU   LC

Conservation Status: Must Exterminate

Description: Physically, the Talking Zombie resembles a Gray Shambler, except for its speed. Most Talking Zombies are dressed as punks, vagrants, petty criminals, and similar members of the urban underclass, although a minority of Talking Zombies appear as buried corpses in tattered dress clothing. This is due to the fact that a number of Talking Zombies arise from the dead buried in cemeteries.

Habits and Habitat: The Talking Zombie is considered the most dangerous species of undead in the world. They possess human or near-human intelligence, above-average speed, and nigh invulnerability. They are highly aggressive predators that actively seek to eat the brains of humans, claiming that it eases the pain of being undead. Even shooting a Talking Zombie in the brain will not kill it. Only total destruction of the body is enough to slay one, and the remains excrete a chemical called trioxin. This chemical is responsible for the genesis of the species.

Talking Zombies prefer to dwell in urban sprawl, where their appearance and odor do not set them apart from the living denizens of such areas. Fortunately, they are usually spree killers, unable to form cogent, long-term plans so outbreaks are easily detected and quarantined.

The greatest danger comes from Talking Zombies that possess a measure of self-control. In several cases, a lone Talking Zombie has survived in a city for months or even years by disguising itself as human and covering its kills in a manner similar to a serial killer. In one known instance, the zombie formed a symbiotic relationship with citizens of a squalid tenement building. In exchange for killing violent criminals and "protecting" the residents from harm, the residents covered up evidence of the zombie's actions and lied to the authorities. Of course, eventually, the zombie lost control when a resident insulted it. The zombie infected every resident in the tenement building except for a lone child and attempted to destroy the entire city in a massive riot. It was finally captured and later destroyed by the police. An unknown number of newly created Talking Zombies escaped.

Reproduction: As with the Gray Shambler, a single bite is enough to infect and transform a human into a Talking Zombie. However, the chemical trioxin can also create a Talking Zombie if exposed to human remains. Even a highly diluted sample of trioxin can animate a corpse. In one tragic case, fallout from the cremation of a single Talking Zombie's corpse led to the animation of an entire graveyard.

The origin of the Talking Zombie is intensely debated. Some believe that the species is artificial, the result of illegal military bio-weapons experimentation. Others contend that the Talking Zombie is the result of pollution, possibly the result of a progenitor serum spill mixed with other chemicals.

Range: Almost every major city in the world is subject to periodic Talking Zombie infestations.

TALKING ZOMBIE
Mortifera immortalis trioxin

An extremely clever and vocal species, this species can successfully negotiate, intimidate, or deceive humans. Despite any possible morals or ethics held while alive, all Talking Zombies are sociopathic, completely lacking empathy for their prey.

The Talking Zombie is unique among the undead in that it actually cares about its appearance. They have been known to style their own hair, change clothing, and wear makeup to appear more lifelike.

Dancing Zombie
Mortifera immortalis choreographicus

EX   ME   CE   VU   LC

Conservation Status: Vulnerable

Description: Lithe animated corpses, typically garbed in fashionable clothing appropriate for dancing. They are only rarely mutilated or in an advanced state of decomposition. The average Dancing Zombie can even be mistaken for a living human under poor lighting conditions. It is only the pallor of their skin that betrays their true identity.

Habits and Habitat: A curious and rare species, the Dancing Zombie is not actually physically dangerous to humans. Instead, troupes of Dancing Zombies will swarm around isolated individuals and subject them to intricate dance numbers. Often when a troupe performs, they will use whatever incidental music is available, typically a nearby radio or stereo system. Victims report being terrified or even thrilled after such an encounter, but no physical harm is reported. Little else is known of their habits or life cycle.

They appear to have some kind of intelligence or awareness of human habits, as the species keeps up with trends in popular dance choreography and fashion. Dancing Zombies have been observed performing everything from traditional folk dances to the latest dance fad.

Some eyewitness accounts have indicated that Dancing Zombies can sing as well as dance. These reports are still unverified. In one case, a witness claimed that two zombies not only sang and danced but acted out a scene from a recent musical. Such "triple threat" zombies could revolutionize the entertainment industry if they were discovered and domesticated.

Reproduction: The most credible theory of the Dancing Zombie's creation compares it to the Revenant. Just as the Revenant is a psychologically motivated zombie species, the Dancing Zombie is similarly motivated by a psychological need. In this case though, Dancing Zombies are driven by a deep need to perform, to draw attention to themselves.

Insecure professional dancers are the prime candidates to become Dancing Zombies, at least in theory. Researchers are still attempting to identify the remains of several Dancing Zombies in an attempt to trace their origins. To date, this effort has not been succcesful.

Range: Presumed to be global. Sightings are few and far between, but they have been encountered in such remote areas as a prison in the Philippines.

DANCING ZOMBIE
Mortifera immortalis choreographicus

Despite their speed and agility, this species has never been known to chase after humans. However, their dancing may be misinterpreted as an act of aggression.

The clothes of the Dancing Zombie are always indicative of their style of dance and are virtually always in good condition and taste. How they find these clothes is a mystery. Some scholars believe finding the origins of their clothes may lead to insight into the species itself.

Western Mall Zombie
Mortifera immortalis consumptus

EX   ME   CE   VU   LC

Conservation Status: Least Concern

Description: A slow and shuffling animated corpse, always dressed in contemporary casual attire suitable for a shopping mall. They are distinguished from Gray Shamblers by their attraction to displays of consumer goods and their much milder odor. A Western Mall's scent is mild and inoffensive, but reports are contradictory as to its exact nature. Many observers claimed it reminded them of "new car smell." It is believed that this odor gives the Western Mall Zombie an advantage when hunting prey in its natural environment, as its scent won't alert unwary victims to its presence until it is too late.

Habits and Habitat: Physiologically similar to the Gray Shambler, this species is obsessed with shopping malls and similar consumerist venues valuing them over hunting grounds. When a Western Mall Zombie is confronted with a display of high end consumer merchandise, it will be lulled into a state of calm.

Many survivors of zombie attacks have lived only after hiding behind a large television or a window display case of the latest fall fashions. It is also possible to lure a horde away through clever use of a PA system or bullhorn. Announcing a sale at a different store will cause the horde to leave its current location and attempt to find the sale. They are easily herded using this technique.

It should be noted that Western Mall Zombies are highly protective and will attack anyone who damages or steals from their territory. They do eat the flesh of the living if it's available but make no great efforts in acquiring it. They clearly value consumer goods and shopping venues above food.

A few corporations have begun experimenting with using the Western Mall Zombie as night guards for shopping malls. They release the zombies at night and lure them into holding pens in the morning. So far, it has proven a highly successful deterrent against theft, but insurance costs might make it impractical as a solution for all shopping malls.

Reproduction: Western Mall Zombies spontaneously mutate out of existing Gray Shamblers. An avid consumer in life who dies after being infected by a Gray Shambler may arise as a Western Mall Zombie instead. The two species are found together. Some may view the Western Mall Zombie as a Gray Shambler that has adapted itself for a specific environment—consumer retail outlets.

Range: Found throughout the world. They prefer suburbia and urban sprawl. Hordes of them will besiege the nearest suitable mall even if it is well protected.

WESTERN MALL ZOMBIE

Mortifera immortalis consumptus

This species is even less perceptive than the Common Shambler. It is also easily distracted by displays of consumer goods.

They are highly possessive of anything they catch, making them a very greedy species.

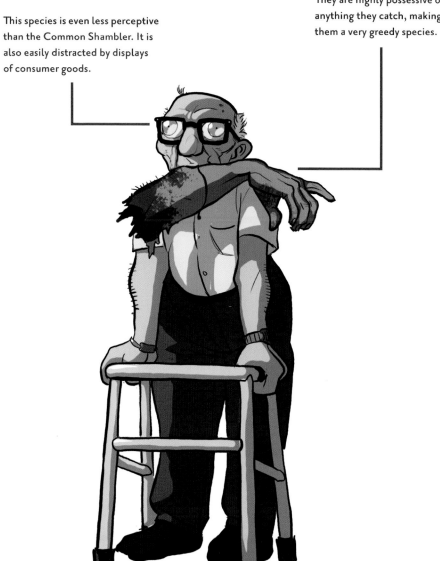

North American Cabin Lurker
Mortifera necronomicus kandarian

EX ME CE VU LC

Conservation Status: Least Concern

Description: The North American Cabin Lurker is characterized by several unique traits: pure white eyes that lack pupils, enlarged jaws and canine teeth, claws instead of fingernails, and the ability to levitate.

Like many other species, the Cabin Lurker was not identified as a member of the *Mortifera* family for many years. Instead, they were mislabeled as serial killers in First World countries or as victims of demonic possession in more superstitious locales. Now researchers have traced this species back to 6,000 BCE, where Sumerian accounts in an ancient religious text known as the *Necronomicon* match their description. The Sumerians called them Kandarian demons and believed that they were a curse from the gods.

Habits and Habitat: Preferring to dwell in isolated forested terrain, Cabin Lurkers spend hours or even days playing with their prey before killing them. Cabin Lurkers are true sadists that possess great cunning and seem to relish inflicting terror on their prey before killing them. It is not uncommon that a Cabin Lurker will play a game of cat and mouse with a single victim until the unfortunate simply passes out from exhaustion. This habit makes them very inefficient hunters, so a Cabin Lurker's body count is typically much lower than its intelligence, speed, and strength would suggest it is capable of achieving.

Reproduction: Interestingly, all known populations of Cabin Lurkers can be traced back to a single source, an archeological dig site of a Sumerian temple in southern Mesopotamia, in what is now Iraq. Throughout the 20th century, archeologists from around the world worked on the site in several major and minor excavations. Whenever the archeologists returned to their home countries with relics or human remains from the dig site for further study, Cabin Lurkers would start to appear. Most of the archeologists in question were the first to undergo transformation or be killed by Cabin Lurkers.

It is now believed that all artifacts from the temple are contaminated with a unique virus that transforms its victims into Cabin Lurkers. The site's exact location is classified and has been quarantined by the World Health Organization. Unfortunately, many relics were smuggled out and sold on the black market before this was learned, so Cabin Lurker infestations still periodically surface. The most dangerous artifact is the *Necronomicon* itself, as it was responsible for the single largest infestation of Cabin Lurkers in history: the infamous 1981 Tennessee U-Mart massacre. Authorities searched extensively for the book, but it is believed that a lone Cabin Lurker took the artifact with it as it searched for new hunting grounds. It has never resurfaced, although rumors place it in various locations around the world.

Range: Global, although they are almost never found far from a Sumerian artifact.

NORTH AMERICAN CABIN LURKER

Mortifera necronomicus kandarian

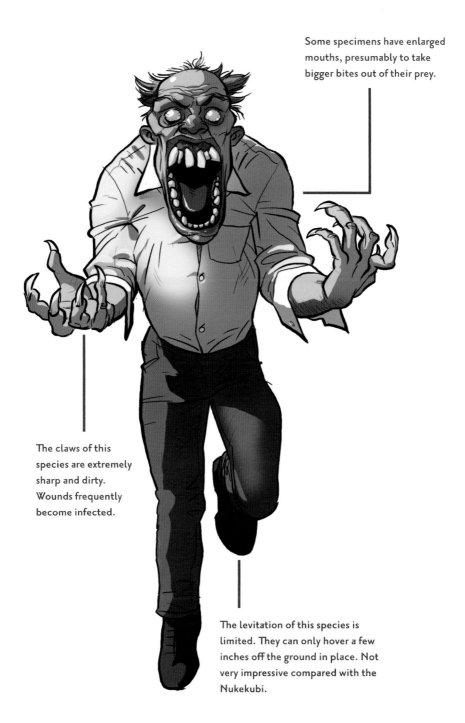

Some specimens have enlarged mouths, presumably to take bigger bites out of their prey.

The claws of this species are extremely sharp and dirty. Wounds frequently become infected.

The levitation of this species is limited. They can only hover a few inches off the ground in place. Not very impressive compared with the Nukekubi.

FLESHLESS ZOMBIE
Mortifera immortalis skeletos

Conservation Status: Critically Endangered

Description: Despite its name, the Fleshless Zombie does have some flesh. The skin of the Fleshless Zombie is gone, sloughed off during the transformation process. Parts of the skeleton can be clearly seen, although the exact pattern of flesh and bone varies with each individual specimen. It is perhaps the most grotesque species of zombie, rivaled only by some Italian Zombies.

Habits and Habitat: Fleshless Zombies are often lone hunters who dwell in isolated areas, picking off potential victims one by one. The horrific sight of a Fleshless Zombie is often enough to paralyze a victim with fear long enough for the zombie to kill or infect its prey. This makes up for the slowness of the species.

Due to its unique physiology, the Fleshless Zombie is extremely slow, even by undead standards. A person could easily outwalk or even crawl away from a Fleshless Zombie, assuming they were not paralyzed in fear. Some researchers have theorized that the Fleshless Zombie could walk at a faster pace but deliberately chooses to walk in a slow and exaggerated manner in order to emphasize its external viscera. The sight of intestines swinging back and forth is grotesque enough to terrorize virtually anyone who witnesses the sight.

Many victims escape a Fleshless Zombie, only to succumb to infection from a minor wound hours or days later. The unsettling sight of the species distracts victims from even realizing that they were harmed by the zombie. This helps the species proliferate, as victims usually travel far before transformation.

Reproduction: As with Gray Shamblers, infection through physical contact. Once a victim begins the transformation process, the skin sloughs off in large chunks over a period of hours. After the transformation is complete, the new zombie begins to hunt for new victims.

Range: Only found in North America and Europe. Not a high-altitude species. Prefers coniferous forests to deciduous. While the distribution is wide, it seems to be common only in forested areas with access to caves and visited by hikers. Though not a communal zombie, ideal habitat can attract multiple individuals. Solitary individuals are easily avoided, but unarmed backpackers should avoid utilizing ledges and caves for shelter, as multiple Fleshless Zombies are problematic and should be considered extremely dangerous.

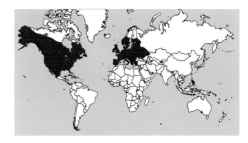

FLESHLESS ZOMBIE
Mortifera immortalis skeletos

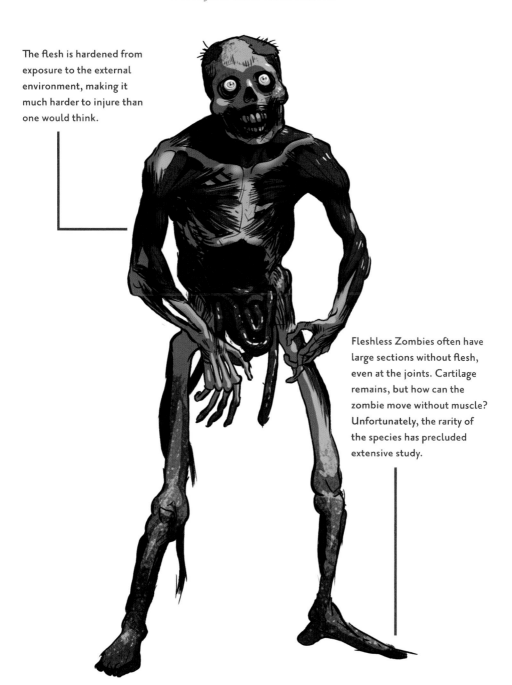

The flesh is hardened from exposure to the external environment, making it much harder to injure than one would think.

Fleshless Zombies often have large sections without flesh, even at the joints. Cartilage remains, but how can the zombie move without muscle? Unfortunately, the rarity of the species has precluded extensive study.

DOMESTICATED GRAY SHAMBLER

Mortifera immortalis servus

Conservation Status: Least Concern

Description: A typical animated corpse, distinguished by their servile behavior towards humans. Typically dressed in work clothes and suffering only from mild to moderate decay, the Domesticated Gray Shambler is seemingly a docile, even timid creature. However, it still possesses the same violent urges of its wild cousins and is prone to lapse into unacceptable behavior.

Habits and Habitat: While zombie domestication is still a hot-button issue in modern society, humans have kept the undead as workers for centuries. Many isolated communities utilized zombies long before it became a talking point among television pundits. For example, some Central Eurasiatic peoples employed Domesticated Gray Shamblers as herdsmen and guards. The tireless dead would watch over livestock while the living villagers slept.

The Domesticated Gray Shambler has evolved into a separate species from its wild cousin. It has a milder temperament than its wild cousins and is generally less aggressive. They can still attack if not managed by a skilled handler.

Best used in work sites without many humans to confuse them, domesticated zombies are simpleminded but dedicated workers. They have been said to labor for years in mines and plantations, even outperforming high-end machinery due to their ability to work nonstop under hazardous conditions. Recently, some have tried to train them as domestic servants, but this is thought to be a bad idea. They are easily confused and enraged by loud or bright stimuli, and most people have no idea how to handle a domesticated zombie. The resulting stress will push the zombie into a feral state, putting everyone at risk.

Reproduction: While the first Domesticated Gray Shamblers were wild-caught zombies, they are now created by human zombie handlers. A handler acquires corpses of humans who have died of non-zombie related causes and then exposes the corpse to a biological sample from an existing Domesticated Shambler, typically a few drops of blood. Within 24 hours of exposure, the corpse arises as a Domesticated Gray Shambler, ready for training.

Range: Global, often found in remote work sites. Like the ubiquitous rock dove (pigeon) or Norway rat, this is a highly adaptable species with few environmental limitations.

DOMESTICATED GRAY SHAMBLER

Mortifera immortalis servus

Traumatic head injuries are a part of domestication training. It is believed by many trainers that one must literally knock some sense into them.

Zombies in customer service jobs are commonly given nicknames by their handlers in order to help put the customer at ease. The Shamblers seem indifferent to this process.

PRETA
Mortifera immortalis gaki

EX   ME   CE   VU   LC

Conservation Status: Critically Endangered

Description: An animated corpse with a distended belly and shrunken frame, similar in appearance to a starving human. Many Preta also have bizarre deformities, such as elongated necks or upside-down faces. Asian folklore mentioning monstrous spirits such as the Yokai are often based on the Preta.

Habits and Habitat: A species on the verge of extinction due to its inability to adapt. Once common in Asian rural settings, the Preta feasted upon isolated farmers and travelers, a glutton with a never-ending appetite. A fast and strong species, the Preta would ambush and devour its victims while they were still alive. An unsuspecting adult male has little chance against this species. However, the Preta were hunted themselves by specialized wandering mercenaries known by a variety of names throughout Asia. These warriors were hired by farming communities or local governments to find and destroy any Preta in the vicinity. This was an extremely dangerous task for even the most talented hunter, but over the generations, they forced the Preta farther and farther from civilization.

It should be noted that many Japanese monks who believed in Esoteric Buddhism considered the Preta to be Sokushinbutsu. The Sokushinbutsu were monks who performed an elaborate ritual suicide to mummify their own body and achieve celestial enlightenment. The ritual took years to complete and involved dosing oneself with small amounts of poison every day in order to make the body inedible to insects. It was believed that the ritual would drive some of the monks insane, causing them to arise as Preta upon completion. Despite their cannibalistic appetites, the monks revered all Sokushinbutsu, even those that turned into Preta. Scientists have discovered thousands of Preta corpses all over Asia, far more than the number of Buddhist monks who attempted the Sokushinbutsu ritual.

Starting in the 20th century, the Preta has been threatened by a dwindling food supply, loss of habitat, and overhunting. While the days of remote villages hiring warriors to protect them from the Preta are long over, many rich game hunters wish to follow in this tradition and pay high prices to hunt the Preta. Furthermore, the gradual loss of rural lands to urban has reduced the places where Preta can hide and hunt. An effort is being made to save the Preta, but its chances are grim. They have not adapted to urban environments as well as other species, and their bizarre deformities make them an easy target to spot.

Reproduction: Preta spontaneously arise from the corpses of greedy and obsessive humans. Contrary to popular belief, a Preta cannot infect a living human with its bite. Of course, few humans survive a bite as the Preta is a dangerous predator.

Range: Asia, primarily in rural and wild environs. Threatened by the rapid urbanization of its native region. Never common, this unusual zombie is suffering the same fate as the tiger. Sadly, in a few decades they may be extirpated from everywhere but the most remote mountain environments. Preservation efforts have been largely ineffective due to a combination of local human antipathy and habitat loss due to the industrialization of its rural habitat.

PRETA

Mortifera immortalis gaki

Over 100 specific deformities unique to the Preta have been catalogued.

The distended belly is similar to a human suffering from starvation, but the Preta is an energetic hunter, despite its appearance.

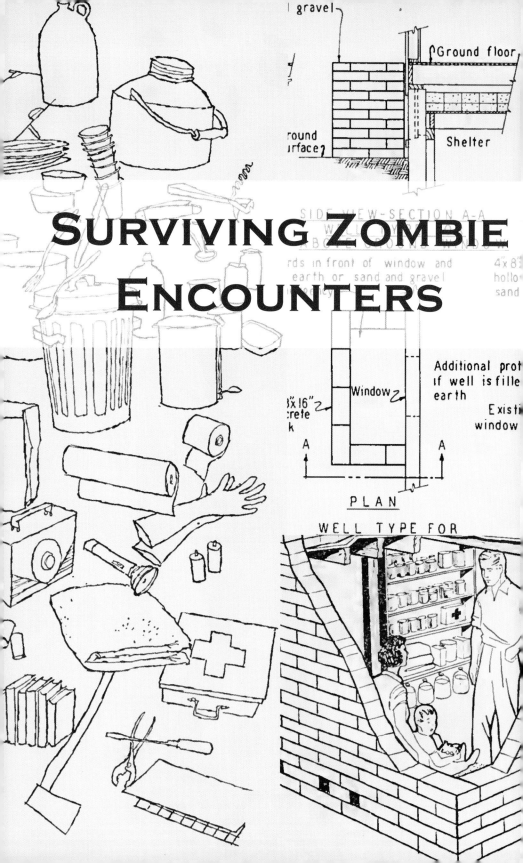

Surviving Zombie Encounters

Encountering one of the undead need not be a dangerous or even unpleasant experience. They are among the most exotic creatures of this planet, and few humans see even a Common Gray Shambler in their lifetime. So-called dead watchers make vacations out of seeing rare zombie species in their native habitats. While many species are apex predators, a bit of common sense and preparation provide a far better protection than any firearm or hastily barricaded house.

Lesson I: Humans Are the Greatest Danger!

In the event of a zombie attack, whether it's a small incursion by a few North American Cabin Lurkers or a large invasion of Common Gray Shamblers, people tend to panic and act on instinct, not reason. If you find yourself under attack, keep your wits and remember the greatest danger comes not from the undead but from fellow survivors. Even people who can be trusted in many other disaster scenarios simply do not cope well with zombies. Others view zombie attacks as an excuse to throw off the shackles of civilization. It is easy to focus on the threat of zombie attacks to the point where you ignore any evidence that your fellow humans pose an even greater danger to you. The corollary to this warning is obvious: survivors are your greatest asset in a zombie attack. Trustworthy humans can mean the difference between life and death in an attack, even if they lack specialized training or equipment. It is far better to stay with a stable civilian than an unstable police officer, especially if the officer is armed. The key skill is identifying which survivors are trustworthy and which are not. This skill is more important than firearms usage, hand-to-hand combat, or first aid. If you don't know who will watch your back in a crisis situation, your odds of getting out alive are slim to none. While most of us will cooperate and help one another, many people simply cannot be trusted. The following survivor types provide examples of what you should beware of in a zombie attack. While some present a clear danger, such as the criminal, others are still dangerous because they can't be relied on in a crisis. Teenagers seldom have the maturity to handle the stress of a zombie attack, and skeptics who deny the existence of zombies clearly have problems with reality. These examples are only a starting point. Ultimately, you must make the decisions yourself. Trust your instincts and best judgment.

Armed Survivalist

Quote: "An armed American is a free American!"

Reason not to trust: Survivalists are by definition trigger-happy conspiracy theorists who fear the government more than the undead. In the event of a zombie attack, they will probably attack law enforcement and other emergency rescue personnel, placing you in danger from the crossfire. Even if they don't antagonize the authorities, survivalists distrust people with mainstream beliefs and may decide that you are part of the problem. It's best to stay away before you come to depend on their guns for protection.

Religious Fanatic

Quote: "The Day of Judgment is at hand! Repent or die!"

Reason not to trust: No matter what faith a fanatic claims to believe in, they all tend to act violently and erratically in a zombie attack. A fanatic might sacrifice themselves to protect dozens of innocent civilians by leading zombies away, or they might decide that all "sinners" are responsible for the undead and lead a mob to execute them. More dangerously, their confidence in their beliefs often places them as leaders in large unorganized groups, since people tend to follow anyone who seems to know what they're doing.

Mentally Ill

Quote: "Mother is fine, she's just a severed head!"

Reason not to trust: Frequently in a zombie attack, strangers are thrown together and must depend on each other to survive the crisis. In times like these, it will be hard to determine if your fellow survivors are merely stressed out or actually insane. If you suspect that a person suffers from a severe mental illness, try to alert trained professionals to take the appropriate steps, or get away from the person.

Criminal

Quote: "You gotta pay if you want protection."

Reason not to trust: A career criminal is a self-centered, amoral, societal parasite by definition. When the thin veneer of civilization is peeled away by a zombie attack, expect the very worst from their ilk. Many criminals are not violent individuals, but they are untrustworthy. Even the nicest crook will abandon you in a moment of danger or may involve you as an accomplice in their own crimes. Looting is a crime, regardless of the circumstances, and being shot by police is just as lethal as a zombie bite.

Unstable Authority Figure

Quote: "I'm in charge, and what I say goes. Or else."

Reason not to trust: Normally in a zombie attack, you should seek out the proper authorities, but stay alert even after finding them. Many officials are not prepared and will crack under the stress of a zombie attack. Typically, the leader becomes insecure about their position and will overcompensate, more concerned with losing their authority than in dealing with the undead. You are just as likely to be shot for disobeying orders as you are to be killed by a zombie.

Skeptic

Quote: "I didn't board up the door, because there's nothing to worry about."

Reason not to trust: Many people can't accept the possibility that the undead might rise up and attack the living. To them, it's something that happens to other people, or in some extreme cases the skeptic refuses to acknowledge the existence of zombies! A skeptic has disconnected from reality and poses a risk to anyone who tries to help them. They could sabotage rescue or zombie defense efforts in an attempt to prove that everyone else is overreacting.

Control Freak

Quote: "Do as I say and no one gets hurt."

Reason not to trust: A control freak has a deep-seated urge to control everyone around them, which will only grow stronger in a crisis. Such a person will do everything in their power to gain leadership of a survivor group and won't tolerate disobedience. Unlike the unstable authority figure, the control freak hasn't cracked. In fact, they probably look forward to a zombie attack, hoping that it would provide them the chance to establish their own kingdom after civilization collapses. To them, other survivors are expendable.

Addict

Quote: "I need my fix."

Reason not to trust: An addict is unable to control their own behavior, and stress tends to increase the craving for another fix – whether it's drugs, alcohol, or something else. Most addicts will focus on ensuring their own needs are fulfilled to the detriment of the group. Even worse, addicts will probably go into withdrawal during the crisis as their personal stash runs out. An addict in this state is extremely dangerous, as they will do anything to get high again, including putting those around them at risk.

Teenager

Quote: "Like, what?"

Reason not to trust: Perhaps the most unreliable of the bunch, teenagers can only be counted on to make bad decisions in a zombie attack. They will run off on their own, show off to impress their peers, and recklessly endanger the group with their stunts, drug usage, and premarital sex. Worse, they don't work well with others, thinking that they know better than the adults. Their decision-making skills are limited at best. They require strict supervision and guidance in a crisis to keep them from getting killed or infected.

People You Can Trust:
Certified Zombie Researchers
and Search-and-Rescue Personnel

Reason to trust: North American Necrological Research Institute (NANRI) certified field researchers and search-and-rescue personnel are capable experts who follow a stringent code of ethics. They put the safety of civilians as their top priority and know how to handle every known species of zombie. Look for the NANRI ID badges and follow their instructions during a crisis. Search-and-rescue teams are on standby to deal with a crisis within 24 hours of detection. If you can survive the first day, your odds of survival improve dramatically.

Lesson 2: What to Do if Confronted by a Zombie

Popular culture depicts zombie slaying as fun, easy, and exciting. Nothing could be further from the truth. In virtually all cases, you should avoid a zombie when confronted. Discretion is the better part of valor. However, you need to keep your wits about you so you can respond to any possible threats you may encounter. Good situational awareness is vital. Don't run from one zombie, because you may be running into the arms of another one. It is easy to find yourself surrounded by the undead while running in a blind panic. You should keep checking for signs of zombies in all directions and respond appropriately.

While fleeing, put as much distance and as many barriers between you and the undead as possible. Distance is better than a barrier, but it is important to put something solid between you and the approaching undead, as you may find yourself cut off from all avenues of escape. It can be as simple as closing and locking a door behind you or knocking a bookcase down on the pursuing zombie.

Once you've identified where the undead are, what species you are confronting and started to flee, you're on the right track to survival. However, you can't always retreat. Humans must rest on occasion, after all. Furthermore, you may find yourself trapped by a zombie or encounter one threatening a loved one. Thus, while fighting the zombie is a measure of last resort, it is sometimes unavoidable.

Firearms are more dangerous to humans than zombies and should not be used unless you have extensive training or have no other choice. A single bullet is highly injurious to a human, no matter where the shot lands, but zombies are barely affected by gunfire, except in certain body parts. Headshots are much harder to make than popular media may lead you to believe. A firearm may inspire a false sense of confidence that will lead you to take risks you would not have taken otherwise and ignore more practical options.

Zombie hand-to-hand combat is a complex topic so we will only address the basics. If you want to learn more, enroll in a zombie defense class or read the definitive primer on the subject, *The Tao of Jiang-Shi-Do* by Lee Jun-Fan.

Learn to improvise: Even trained martial artists are at a disadvantage when facing a zombie in unarmed combat. Instead, use whatever is at hand to fight the zombie. A chair can be used to push a zombie away, a rag can be stuffed in the mouth of a zombie to keep it from biting, and a hammer can deliver a blow to the skull. Don't be afraid to break things in order to survive. More than one victim of an attack hesitated when given the chance to use a valuable item to fight off a zombie and paid the ultimate price in doing so.

Keep your distance: Stay as far away as you can from the undead in a confrontation. Even in a hand-to-hand fight, try to keep the zombie from grappling you. The undead want to get as close as possible so they can bite and claw freely.

Aim for the legs: Killing a zombie is harder than you might think, but disabling one is much easier. If you can knock out a zombie's knees, you will be able to flee or dispatch it safely. Not applicable to specimens that lack legs.

Too much force is not enough: Don't hold back when fighting the undead. Use as much force as you can in each attack. Zombies are resilient creatures so an attack that would be lethal to a human might only be an inconvenience to the undead. This ties in with improvisation. A car isn't just a mode of transportation. It's a deadly weapon capable of generating tremendous amounts of kinetic force to a target. Don't worry about the resale value of your sedan when a Fleshless Zombie is menacing your family. Their lives are infinitely more valuable than the car. Similarly, power tools and caustic chemicals are worth using, but be wary of hurting yourself or others as well. As with firearms, these weapons are more dangerous to yourself than the zombie if mishandled.

Lesson 3: Flee, Don't Fight!

In general, your safety depends on avoiding direct contact with the undead. Over half of all zombie-related deaths are caused by untrained civilians trying to fight a zombie. When in doubt, flee from the undead and contact the authorities. Stockpiling weapons, gathering around other scared civilians in a badly barricaded structure is a surefire recipe for disaster. Hysteria and group dynamics will almost always lead to poor decision-making, which compromises the safety of everyone involved. Before you flee, you should learn how to identify when zombies are nearby. This is trickier than it appears. Zombies do not always stand out, moaning and shuffling to announce their presence. Often, they will be hard to spot until it's too late. The five senses are all you need to detect the undead before it's too late.

Smell: Virtually all species of undead have a strong pungent odor: the scent of rotting flesh. If you find the smell is growing stronger, stop and look where you're going. You are probably headed towards an unseen zombie.

Taste: Believe it or not, taste can help warn you of nearby zombies. We do not recommend licking or tasting a zombie, as each species is considered unfit for human consumption. However, food and water that has been in the presence of a zombie changes, becoming more bitter than before. The change may be subtle, but it can alert you to undead in the area.

Sight: A zombie in plain sight is easily identified, but you should be more concerned with what you aren't seeing. Be very careful around built-up areas that offer many concealed positions from which a zombie could attack a passerby. Every blind spot is a hazard that should be avoided if at all possible. If you must pass a blind spot, move quickly.

Sound: Some species are quite noisy with their moans and shuffling. Others are very quiet, but no species is completely silent. Listen for sounds that indicate the presence of a zombie and pay attention to what sounds you don't hear. Many animals are afraid of zombies and do not make a sound when in the presence of the undead. The absence of bird calls or dogs barking is a warning sign.

Touch: Many species leave physical traces as they move through an environment and it may not always be practical to trust your sight alone, so feel around to find the traces. These traces are typically either pieces of the zombie itself or mold growing on the undead. When a zombie scrapes against a hard surface it leaves traces behind. Physically touching the ground is a vital step in detecting zombies in areas such as urban settings or areas with low visibility. While it is disgusting, touch is a more precise sense than sight, as every species has a unique texture.

NANRI has a video educational kit called "I Touched A Zombie: A Tactile Identification Guide." The kit offers simulated samples of commonly found species, while the educator's kit offers actual samples of zombies for touching. (The educator's kit requires a class III biohazard handling license to purchase.)

SMELL

TASTE

SIGHT

SOUND

TOUCH

Lesson 4: Know the Law

Federal and state law still applies in the event of a zombie attack. Destroying a protected zombie that poses no threat to human life can land you in legal trouble, and recklessly endangering the lives of others is always a crime. State laws vary, but most follow the same general principles:

Report all wild zombie sightings to the authorities. It is not necessary to call in a domesticated zombie at work, but even a single Common Gray Shambler should be reported to the police or local NANRI branch. While failure to report is not always a crime (it varies from state to state), it is a good idea regardless.

It is only legal to destroy ME (Must Exterminate) species or individual zombies currently threatening other humans. ME species are by their very nature considered an ongoing threat to human life, so they are always "open season." Deciding if a zombie is threatening human life can be a snap judgment that doesn't always turn out right. The law recognizes this, but it is not permissible to provoke attacks from zombies in an attempt to justify their destruction.

It is illegal to destroy a zombie that poses no threat to human life. Some species are inherently nonthreatening, such as the Dancing Zombie. Others only attack if severely provoked, such as the Domesticated Gray Shambler. You will be prosecuted if you overreact to the presence of a zombie.

You must report all zombie-related injuries to the authorities. Failure to report zombie-related injuries is a severe crime and a public health hazard. Not all zombie injuries are fatal, and recent advances in treatment could give you a good chance of survival from wounds that would have been lethal only a few years ago. If you conceal an injury from knowledgeable authorities, you put not only your own life in danger but also the lives of everyone around you.

It is illegal to capture zombies or store their remains without a license. Taking a "souvenir" is dangerous and in poor taste. While there is a thriving black market for zombie body parts and live zombies, trafficking in zombies is illegal and punishable with lengthy prison sentences.

Lesson 5: Prepare Now!

Despite the many popular media stories of a so-called zombie apocalypse, it is all but impossible for the undead to destroy civilization or humanity. However, many people are attacked by zombies every year, and learning how to protect yourself can mean the difference between life or death.

Take a zombie defense class: As mentioned in lesson 2, many martial arts schools offer zombie hand-to-hand defense classes that teach useful skills for surviving a zombie attack, such as barehanded defense, grappling, and escaping the grip of a zombie. Advanced students might look into learning parkour or free running – a form of gymnastics that emphasizes moving through difficult terrain quickly. An expert in parkour can easily avoid zombie hordes by climbing and running over and around them.

Watch the news: Media outlets are required by federal law to report zombie outbreaks and attacks. By knowing where and when the undead have attacked, you will know to prepare ahead of time. Rely only on sources with a good reputation for accuracy. Many news sources are too eager to report every rumor without bothering to confirm them.

Figure out whom you can trust: Other people are the greatest threat you face in a zombie attack. Assess each of your friends and associates and determine whom you would trust with your life in the event of a crisis.

Don't become obsessed: It's easy to become seduced by the zombie-survivalist industry and think that buying the right weapon or transforming your home into a fortress will keep you safe. Multiple case studies show that survivalists fare only slightly better than the average person and do far worse than someone who only spends a moderate amount of time preparing for zombie attacks. This is because other people tend to target survivalists in a crisis, looking to steal their stockpile of weapons and supplies, not realizing that survivalists often do not cooperate with others in attacks. This lack of trust dooms them to dying alone surrounded by army surplus rations and hollowpoint bullets, and under attack by zombies or desperate looters.

Lesson 6: Know the Undead

Learn about the zombie species that live around you. Whenever you encounter a zombie, contact NANRI to identify its species so you can better prepare for any possible encounters in the future.

Knowing the difference between what a Talking Zombie and an Italian Zombie can do may mean the difference between life and death, as each species hunts for prey differently. Some species of zombie have very selective habits and may not pose a threat to you. Learning how to react to each species is vital.

For example, a Revenant only hunts the people it believes are responsible for its death, but it will defend itself against anyone who threatens it. Attacking a Revenant that has nothing to do with you decreases your chances of survival. Attacking zombies without understanding which species they are and what motivates them is a common, but deadly, mistake.

Bear in mind that some species pose no threat to humans. For instance, there has never been a recorded case of a Dancing Zombie killing a human. At worst, Dancing Zombies have injured humans with misplaced kicks during a dance routine. Thus, they are best left alone. Adopting a "better safe than sorry" approach and killing them is not a good idea. It would almost certainly waste time, energy, and bullets better saved for actual threats. Other, more deadly zombies may be lured to the area by the noise and attack. Finally, there may be legal repercussions from killing harmless undead.

Knowledge of the undead also tends to calm survivors during a crisis. If you can demonstrate that you understand zombies, other survivors will turn to you for guidance and advice. This helps to prevent hysteria and panic, essential in a zombie attack.

Learning the basic traits of commonly encountered species is a key survival skill. Start by reading all of the entries in this field guide carefully and familiarizing yourself with them. That should be enough to help you distinguish between extremely dangerous species, such as the North American Cabin Lurker, and less threatening ones. Once you know what you're dealing with, you will know how to respond appropriately.

A Social History
of the Undead

As the zombie has been part of our world for countless millennia, every society that has come into contact with the undead has had to respond to their actions. Most cultures reacted violently, treating the zombie as a threat to be exterminated without exception. This shortsighted policy served well enough in earlier times, but now as our civilization becomes more advanced, we have recognized that even the lowly zombie is valuable and worth protecting.

In order to understand our current beliefs about the undead, we should examine our historical attitudes towards zombies. In brief, we can divide our history into five periods: ancient, medieval, early modern, the zombie rights movement, and contemporary. Each period viewed the zombie with a unique perspective.

Above right: The Aztecs worshipped Aztec Mummies, regularly offering human sacrifices to them. The mummies also enjoyed throwing humans into pits filled with snakes.

Below right: The Spanish brought invasive species that preyed upon Aztec Mummies. Chronologically Displaced Robots were especially devastating, as they used the mummies as fuel.

Ancient: The Zombie as Demon (7000 BCE – 500 CE)

For most of humanity's history, the zombie has largely been regarded as a demon straight from the pits of hell, a malevolent being acting on the orders of a greater supernatural authority. Because of the theological implications, the policies of ancient societies were often bizarre and contradictory to our modern sensibilities, but the people of those times took the undead very seriously. To them, zombies represented a threat to the mind, body, and soul.

Most ancient civilizations, from Sumerian to Roman, viewed the undead as a sign of divine or infernal anger. Priests or shamans were required to uncover its source and determine how to ease the anger. As interpreters of the unseen world, priests wielded considerable power in setting zombie policy, but even the most zealous holy man saw the need to be reasonable in his decisions. After all, a priest's power resided in the faith of his followers. If the masses were not sufficiently reassured that the priest could protect them, they would soon abandon their faith.

Typically, the priest would point to some common sin in society as the cause and would bless a group of warriors to dispatch the undead. Warriors who were wounded in battle were executed, as their injuries were proof that they had sinned or were otherwise unclean. This basic template was followed by clerics of many religions. For examples of this pattern, compare the accounts of Buddhist monks blessing

the soldiers of Emperor Hongwu in 1370 CE before they purged a remote village of Preta to the priests of Apollo at Delphi blessing warriors before purging one of the sporadic flare-ups of Shamblers in ancient Greece. Both accounts follow the same pattern, right down to the execution of injured combatants at its conclusion. Some folklorists have used this pattern to explain why certain myth structures are found throughout the world, pointing to commonalities between the historical accounts and folklore. If you wish to learn more about the connection between historical zombie attacks and folklore, read Fran Von Junzt's book *Hades at Our Doorstep: The Undead and Mythology.*

It should be noted that a few exceptions to this pattern can be found. Often when dealing with species with unusual behavioral habits, such as the Dancing Zombie, the clergy would come up with highly unorthodox policies. For example, judging from the few Aztec codices still in existence, we believe that the Aztec Mummy was a sacrosanct creature and often a guest of honor at human sacrifice rituals. Even though the Aztec Mummy did attack humans, they were ordered to be left alone, under penalty of death.

Above: Aztec Mummies were not afraid of humans because the native people worshipped them or left them alone. When the Spanish arrived, they were unprepared for their lethal response.

Thankfully for the populace, Aztec Mummies preferred to dwell in isolated areas and temples tended by priests who could safely interact with them. It is believed that the policy was not only enacted for theological reasons but pragmatic ones as well: the Aztec Mummies were feared by enemies of the Aztec empire, and it is thought that the Aztec leadership could herd groups of the undead at strategic choke points in order to halt an enemy's army. Of course, this theory does not explain why the Aztecs failed to use the mummies against Spanish conquistadors. Perhaps invasive species such as the Chronologically Displaced Robot (*Talos tempus viator*) introduced by the Spanish had already driven them away.

Middle Ages & Renaissance
(500 – 1700 CE)

After the Roman Empire fell and Christianity began to spread through Europe, humanity came into contact with the undead more frequently than ever before. Scholars are unsure why the undead population spiked in this era. While we will never know for certain how often ancient man encountered the undead, it was probably a rare event. There is little evidence suggesting that ancient civilizations suffered from many zombie attacks. While some villages and cities undoubtedly fell to the undead, ancient societies could go decades or even centuries between attacks. Scholars have offered many theories as to why the ancient world was relatively free of zombie hordes, but all agree that the zombie was not a serious threat to civilization until the Middle Ages.

It is in this age that we first read accounts of zombie hordes laying siege to walled cities and fortresses, depopulating the countryside, and threatening humanity with extinction. Physical evidence is plentiful as well. Archeologists have uncovered battlefields where armored knights battled huge numbers of the undead, far larger than any ancient zombie-human conflict. Excavations of sites where medieval villages once stood have revealed similarly devastating attacks. Scholars have determined that zombie populations rose dramatically in the Middle Ages, particularly in regions ravaged by war or plague. Inevitably, these zombies came into contact with humanity, usually with violence.

The rise in apocalyptic beliefs in the Middle Ages can be partially accounted for by this unprecedented rise in zombie-human conflicts. It is no surprise that a group of mystics and zealots formed to observe and understand the undead. What is surprising is that this group, the Silens (Silent), lasted for centuries as a minor heretical movement before being suppressed by the church and produced some of the most important written records regarding the undead in this time.

Members of the Silens were usually disaffected monks or educated aristocrats with an interest in the occult and alchemy. As devout Christians, they struggled to reconcile their beliefs with the fact that the undead existed and preyed upon the faithful and heathen equally. The official explanations provided by the church did not satisfy them. They met in secret to theorize how zombies fit into God's plan for the universe. Their beliefs took an apocalyptic bent, as they decided that zombies were proof that the End Times were drawing near. As they drew from various mystic texts and apocryphal books of the Bible, they created an elaborate cosmology in which zombie-related events were portents sent from God. In order to understand the meaning behind the portent, the Silens had to record each and every event they learned of, so they could better understand what God wanted of them. Just as early astrologers made the first accurate astronomical observations, the Silens became the first true scholars of the undead.

The greatest work of the Silens was a collection of zombie observations. Nicknamed the Silens Domesday, it is a series of books that catalogues thousands of zombie events and observations, not just attacks but sightings and peaceful interactions between human and undead. Thirty-nine volumes of the Silens Domesday have been found, although more are suspected to exist. The Silens believed that each encounter had a cosmic significance that could be learned by interpreting the event with numerology and other forms of divination. For example, a charcoal burner that sees a lone Revenant in a forest supposedly foretells of good hunting for the next fortnight, while a knight slain by a Draugr is an omen of war. Many nobles paid handsomely for predictions and advice for dealing with zombies, as the Silens learned a great deal of practical information as well. They were the first to realize that zombies came in a multitude of species, as they correctly identified Revenants, Draugrs, Italian Zombies, and of course Shamblers.

The Silens were eventually declared heretics by the Vatican and their members scattered to the winds. Most of their work was burned but many volumes were saved by occultists and alchemists. Some thought that the secrets of the undead were crucial in uncovering the philosopher's stone of alchemical legend. In any case, the secrets of the Silens did not become public knowledge until 1937 when professors from Miskatonic University republished three volumes of the Silens Domesday. Since then, scholars from around the world have sought out additional volumes, as a new find brings great prestige to the discoverer.

Early Modern: The Zombie as Public Health Hazard (1700 – 1900)

As the Enlightenment began in Europe, people questioned the assumptions made about zombies in earlier times. Instead of assuming they were the products of a supernatural world, visionaries and scholars realized they were products of the natural world and subject to the laws of science. Early scientists were eager to learn the laws that governed the actions of zombies. Many lives were lost in their eager but crudely conducted experiments.

Little headway was made in these experiments, as early researchers lacked the necessary understanding of the natural sciences to comprehend the physiological and biological data they gathered. However, their observations on the behavior of the undead were invaluable. In particular, one English scholar, Laban Shrewsbury, documented more than a hundred zombie outbreaks in the British Isles from 1713 to 1736 in his *Accounts of Revenant Excursions*. While written descriptions of undead attacks were commonplace by then, Shrewsbury was unique in that he went to great lengths to gather quantitative data, such as the number of zombies involved, the length of attack, and the speed of the spread of infection. With this information, other early scientists developed the first effective public health policies to combat the spread of zombies. The Royal Society made Shrewsbury a Fellow for his work, and his book is recognized as the first practical exploration of the zombie as a scientific subject.

By declaring the zombie a public health hazard instead of a sign of divine anger, people were motivated to take proactive steps against outbreaks rather than merely reacting to them.

Due to the poor understanding of the mechanics behind zombie infection, the first policies were often too severe or too mild. A law in 1814 Prussia required that any village that suffered a single fatality by a zombie had to be quarantined for a year. Napoleon had villages burned to the ground after suffering a mild outbreak, while Spain's King Ferdinand failed to contain a major outbreak of the undead in 1810 because it occurred on the land of a favored advisor and the king did not want to embarrass him by sending troops in to clean it up.

Despite these setbacks, progress marched on, and as science improved, so did our comprehension of the undead. Acceptance of the germ theory of disease was invaluable in developing effective methods for stopping zombie outbreaks. Scientists began to correctly identify disease vectors, such as bite wounds from a zombie. By the start of the Civil War, zombies were considered a public health hazard that had to be remedied with rational techniques and strong leadership. Confederate and Union leaders both discussed the possibility of weaponizing zombies, but the idea was rejected – with one notable exception. A Confederate guerrilla leader named Cullen Ward smuggled Common Gray Shamblers into St. Louis, resulting in a widespread infection that plagued the region for months until it was finally stamped out. Ward was eventually lynched for his actions. The public health hazard theory went unchallenged until 1872, when a young scientist named Amery Smith talked to a New England Ghoul named Byron for the first time.

Smith discovered the ghoul named Byron in the sewers of London. He was charting the sewers in an attempt to study possible zombie attack paths. To his surprise, Byron apologized for startling him and offered to guide him to a nearby manhole. Astonished that a zombie could talk, Smith interviewed the ghoul, a conversation that lasted for hours. Byron insisted that he was a pacifist who only fed upon homeless who had died of natural causes; he had lived for centuries. Smith visited the creature several times before persuading him to come to the surface. The ghoul was immediately captured by several agents in the employ of Smith. Soon after that, Smith began a sideshow exhibition displaying the infamous "Spring Heeled Jack – famed monster of London!"

Above: Pirates unintentionally helped to spread zombies around the world by employing "deadshot" to terrorize enemies in battle. Surprisingly, many of the zombies fired from cannon survived long enough to make it to the closest land mass.

While at first the public was horrified by the ghoul, Byron's strange charm won over the masses of London. The people saw the ghoul not as a monster to be feared or hated but as a harmless oddity. The exhibit was renamed *Meet Melmoth the Wanderer*, and members of the audience were allowed to ask "Melmoth" questions about history for a small fee. Byron's humble nature, eloquent speech, and honesty endeared him to the working poor who made up the majority of the audience. The ghoul became a mascot of sorts to the downtrodden factory workers, petty criminals, and other undesirables of London.

After several months of poor treatment, Byron was taken by the British government, concerned about the possibility of an outbreak of ghoulism. Before Byron could be put down, a riot broke out when Smith announced to the queued up visitors that the Crown had seized "Melmoth" and intended to execute him. Incensed that their favorite performer had been arrested, the mob cried out for the ghoul's release and easily overwhelmed the constables on hand. Believing that the government had sent Byron to the Tower of London, the mob attempted to storm the fortress. The garrison at the

Tower was ordered to repel the mob by any means necessary, resulting in a bloody massacre. Thirty-three were killed in the riot, including Amery Smith, who was found stabbed near the Tower of London. The government claimed that Byron escaped, aided by unknown accomplices, but many conspiracy theorists think that Byron was whisked away to a secret lab to serve as a lab animal in a government project to learn the secrets of immortality. The truth behind Byron the Ghoul may never be known.

Byron became an icon of the era and a popular topic for debate among the intellectuals of the day. His existence proved that not all undead were mindless beasts that threatened everyone around them. His intelligence disproved the belief that the mind could not survive the transformation into undeath and opened a new avenue of scientific query: could the zombification process be perfected, granting humans immortality without any of the disadvantages of being undead? As a result of these new discussions, some voices of reason emerged by the turn of the century, pointing out that at least some zombies must be protected. These voices remained isolated until the founding of the Osiris Club, the first organization dedicated to the preservation and study of the zombie in 1892.

Modern: The Zombie as Endangered Species (1892 – 1980)

As society's view of the undead grew more nuanced, many thinkers sought to utilize zombies for humanity's benefit. Of course, the Haitian and Domesticated Gray Shambler species had long been used in limited numbers; scientists and engineers rushed to industrialize the rest of the undead. Unfortunately, the earliest attempts were fraught with danger and moral dilemmas. The most infamous project, the Dexter Factory, became the center of a national controversy after an exposé, The Abattoir, was published in 1906.

Left: Portrait of "Melmoth" by an unknown artist, circa 1872. Despite his appearance, the ghoul impressed London crowds with his intellect and wit.

Written by an unknown author using the pseudonym of Anthony Quine, The Abattoir is ostensibly a novel about an unnamed factory making use of experimental quickened workers dressed in rubber suits that completely conceal them. As the novel progresses, it becomes apparent that the workers are actually zombies dressed in suits that have been vacuumed of all air so as to prevent decay-causing bacteria from growing. Due to the owner's demand for increased productivity, the few human employees are forced to manage an ever-growing number of undead workers in a dangerous industrial workplace with predictable results. Some are killed by errant zombies, but many more die in horrible industrial accidents, mangled and maimed by machinery designed without a single thought to the safety of those operating it. Several characters are murdered for attempting to unionize by thugs in the employ of the unseen owner. In the novel's finale, the factory catches fire, releasing thousands of suit-clad zombies into the nearby slums. It is only then revealed that the factory was a cannery, and millions of unsuspecting citizens around the nation had eaten food prepared by the undead.

Soon after the novel's publication, reporters from several newspapers in Chicago wrote that the novel was a true story based on a cannery owned by Charles Dexter, a prominent businessman and political boss. Dexter had covered up the deaths and release of the zombies, but the novel finally revealed the truth. Fortunately, the zombies themselves did not kill anyone, as their suits prevented them from biting.

The outcry produced by the controversy led to some of the first worker safety and food inspection laws in the country. More importantly, the first commercial zombie regulations were passed in order to prevent possible contamination in the food supply, even though no outbreaks or infections were ever reported as a result of the Dexter Factory.

The new regulations slowed down but did not stop efforts to make the undead a part of the economic cycle. Entrepreneurs found ways to use the undead in limited roles, mostly dangerous or distasteful industrial jobs that no human wanted to do. This led to a massive drop in wild zombie populations, as poachers sought to capture as many zombies of all species as possible to sell to opportunistic businessmen. The rapid depletion of zombies led to shortages and rumors of grisly "dead farms," where hapless travelers and homeless people were forcibly infected so they could be sold as industrial workers. This urban legend has never been proven, yet it still persists today, as evidenced by recent chain emails.

Interestingly, the first steps to protect the undead from extinction came from early wildlife preservationists. Drake Island, a remote nature preserve off the coast of Florida established in 1880, suffered from frequent poaching.

Right: The Hula Ghouls of World War II became a popular subject in pulp fiction after the war. Several films and novels make use of them. They are credited with making zombies more acceptable in the public eye, an instrumental factor in the passage of important zombie legislation.

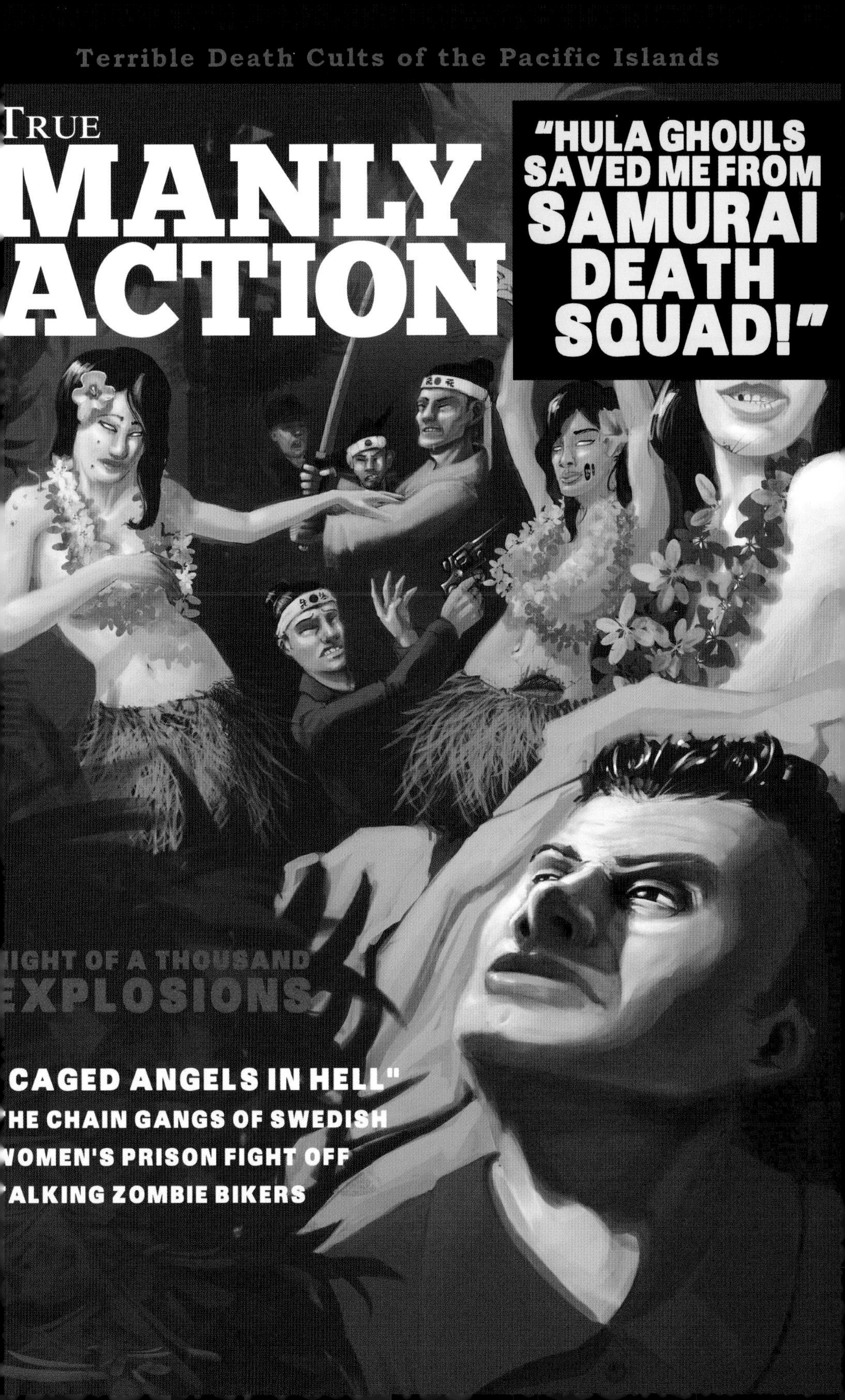
Terrible Death Cults of the Pacific Islands
TRUE
MANLY
ACTION
"HULA GHOULS SAVED ME FROM SAMURAI DEATH SQUAD!"
IGHT OF A THOUSAND
EXPLOSIONS
CAGED ANGELS IN HELL"
HE CHAIN GANGS OF SWEDISH
OMEN'S PRISON FIGHT OFF
ALKING ZOMBIE BIKERS

At that time, the government could not afford to take adequate measures to protect the preserve so a group of environmentalists decided to take an unusual measure to protect Drake Island. They imported several Draugrs from Europe and let them roam free on the island. In order to place the zombies on the island, the preservationists classified them as an endangered species. The Draugrs made short work of any poachers who made landfall. While the measure was controversial, it proved to be incredibly effective. The island was renamed Draugr Island and today is considered the most pristine wildlife preserve in the United States.

As the zombie rights movement grew in prominence, a backlash of anti-zombie hatred arose. While the scientific community had long since accepted that the undead were a valuable part of the natural world, anti-zombie reactionaries irrationally lashed out at anything associated with zombies. Some were motivated by religion, still believing that the undead were a plague sent by the devil. Others had personal motives, having lost family members to zombie attacks. A few were simply psychotic and enjoyed killing without having to face criminal penalty. Illegal hunting parties exterminated countless zombies for decades even when the undead did not pose any kind of threat to humanity. The government ignored the anti-zombie groups until 1946, allowing them to flourish nationwide. They would regret this move, as zombies became part of the West's Cold War strategy and national sentiment had become friendlier to zombies since the Hula Ghouls of World War II.

For reasons unknown, a troupe of Dancing Zombies known as the Hula Ghouls (a misnomer, as Dancing Zombies are not a species of ghoul) followed Americans in the Pacific campaign during World War II and acted to save the lives of hundreds of Allied service members. Dressed as Hawaiian hula girls, the Dancing Zombies often intervened in battle to distract Japanese infantry by performing a hula dance around them. Despite their training and battle-hardened experience, the Japanese often froze at the sight of the Hula Ghouls, inexplicably terrified at the sight of Dancing Zombies in grass skirts. Of course, many times the distraction did not work and the Hula Ghouls were destroyed by machine gun fire. Still, they became a good-luck charm to the Allies in the Pacific and changed the attitudes of millions, as they became a hit in American newsreels. Their

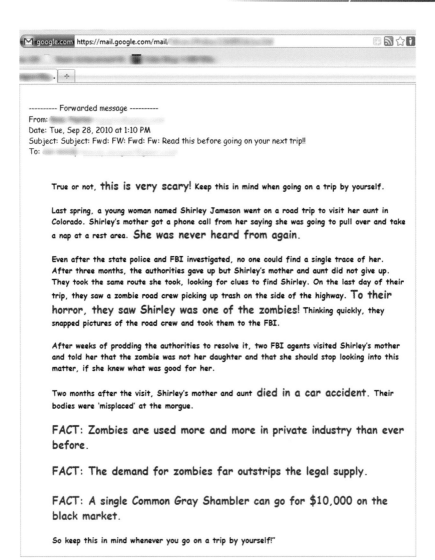

----------- Forwarded message ----------
From:
Date: Tue, Sep 28, 2010 at 1:10 PM
Subject: Subject: Fwd: FW: Fwd: Fw: Read this before going on your next trip!!
To:

True or not, this is very scary! Keep this in mind when going on a trip by yourself.

Last spring, a young woman named Shirley Jameson went on a road trip to visit her aunt in Colorado. Shirley's mother got a phone call from her saying she was going to pull over and take a nap at a rest area. She was never heard from again.

Even after the state police and FBI investigated, no one could find a single trace of her. After three months, the authorities gave up but Shirley's mother and aunt did not give up. They took the same route she took, looking for clues to find Shirley. On the last day of their trip, they saw a zombie road crew picking up trash on the side of the highway. To their horror, they saw Shirley was one of the zombies! Thinking quickly, they snapped pictures of the road crew and took them to the FBI.

After weeks of prodding the authorities to resolve it, two FBI agents visited Shirley's mother and told her that the zombie was not her daughter and that she should stop looking into this matter, if she knew what was good for her.

Two months after the visit, Shirley's mother and aunt died in a car accident. Their bodies were 'misplaced' at the morgue.

FACT: Zombies are used more and more in private industry than ever before.

FACT: The demand for zombies far outstrips the legal supply.

FACT: A single Common Gray Shambler can go for $10,000 on the black market.

So keep this in mind whenever you go on a trip by yourself!"

Above: A common chain email forwarded millions of times over the years, despite being disproven. Urban legends and misinformation still shape public perceptions of the undead, despite the great advances we have made in understanding zombies.

heroism during the war remains unexplained to this day, but folk legend reports that the attack on Pearl Harbor angered the spirits of Hawaii, causing them to send forth a plague of the undead on their enemy.

After World War II, the zombie rights movement became influential enough to convince the federal government to crack down on anti-zombie violence when it was not connected to self-defense or sound wildlife management policy. For the first time in modern history, zombies were not fair game all the time. People had to demonstrate a reason to dispatch the undead or face fines or even jail time. This set off a nationwide debate on the role of zombies in our world.

By the 1960s, civil unrest over "the zombie question" had sparked riots and mass disturbances around the country. Pro- and anti-zombie activists clashed in the streets, while legislators sought to find a balance between the two extremes. Interestingly, zombie attacks spiked dramatically, culminating in the summer of 1968, when thousands of zombie attacks were reported around the country. In an effort to quell the social unrest, the government passed a series of laws aimed at protecting the undead as a strategic military asset against the Soviet Union. Project RESURRECTIONIST, a program aimed at weaponizing the undead, began in 1968 as a result. This compromise did not fully satisfy either side, but the violence finally subsided.

In 1973, the Endangered Zombie Protection Act was passed by Congress as a comprehensive set of rules to regulate how zombies are treated. Its major effect was to specify which zombie species should be classified as endangered and what level of protection they should be afforded. There are five levels of classification: common, vulnerable, critically endangered, extinct, and must exterminate. The last level is reserved only for species considered so dangerous that they must be destroyed on sight. While the act is controversial to this day, it has become the foundation of contemporary zombie policy not only in the United States but around the world. Dozens of other countries have passed laws modeled on the act, and it has become the foundation of contemporary zombie policy.

Today

The zombie's future is still uncertain. Many species are extinct, such as the Aztec Mummy. Other species face threats from a rapidly changing environment; a growing human population; and reinvigorated efforts by anti-zombie reactionaries, poachers, and extremists to annihilate all undead. Organizations such as the Osiris Club and NANRI strive to protect and study the undead, and several zombie preserves have been established to safeguard endangered species. Ultimately, it is up to all of us to ensure that we learn how to coexist peacefully with our undead brethren, as they may well hold the keys to our future.

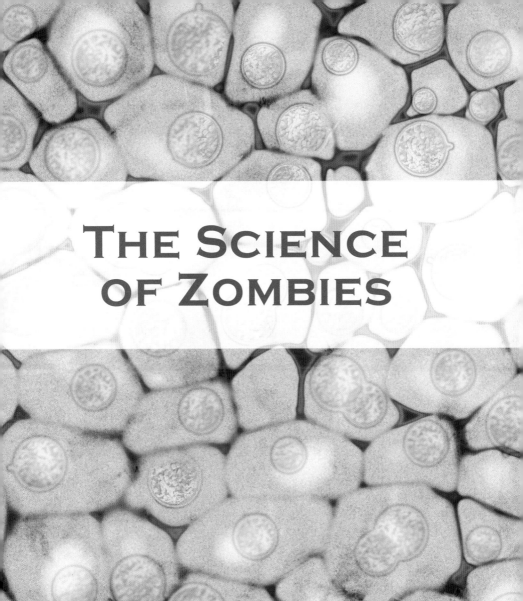

THE SCIENCE
OF ZOMBIES

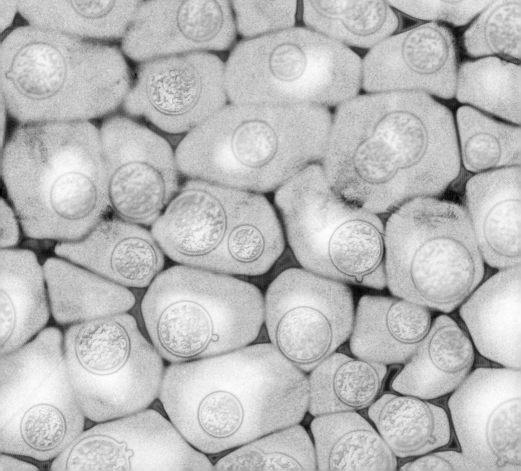

Delving into the secrets of the undead is one of the world's fastest growing industries. While legislation in the United States (crafted by politicians more concerned with winning the votes of superstitious citizens than helping all of mankind) has hindered cutting-edge necrological research, teams in foreign countries have made startling advances in the field.

Research focuses on four major fields; renewable energy, medical applications, intelligence and domestication studies, and longevity. Each area offers limitless potential benefits to humanity if only we make the necessary changes to the legal system to fully protect the undead from extinction and allow researchers unlimited freedom in their pursuit of knowledge. Of the four fields, renewable energy shows the most immediately realizable benefits.

Renewable Energy

The mystery of the *Omega Anima* is of great interest to researchers not only because of the challenges it presents but because of its potential practical applications. If we were to learn how to tap into the same energy source that gives the undead their endless strength, it should be theoretically possible to derive energy from it. Initial studies into this field have already generated exciting results, albeit in an unusual manner.

Dead Run, a NANRI zombie-kinetic test power station, is the first of its kind – a functioning generator utilizing only the undead to generate two megawatts of clean electricity. This is accomplished by chaining several thousand zombies to pedal generators, similar in appearance and function to stationary bicycles. The zombies are attached to the machines so that when they try to shamble or run, they move the pedals. Each zombie generates an average of 200 watts of electricity and more importantly requires no food or rest. The greatest difficulty lies in getting the zombies to keep moving.

In order to motivate the undead, scientists have experimented with many different kinds of stimuli, ranging from plastic toy brains dangling from sticks to live actors screaming and pantomiming the act of running away from the undead. So far, no magic bullet has been found. It seems that even individual members of the same species will react differently to motivational stimuli. In general, the more

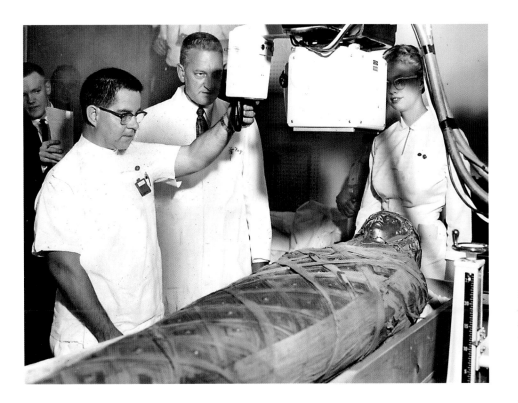

Above: NANRI researchers X-ray an Egyptian Mummy as part of Project RESURRECTIONIST. It laid the foundations of modern zombie studies.

Next Page: The Dead Run power station working at full capacity. Engineers are still trying to perfect the process for mass power generation, experimenting to see what stimuli works most effectively on the zombies.

dangerous and violent species, such as the Talking Zombie (*Mortifera immortalis trioxin*) and the Revenant (*Mortifera reverto vorheesi*), are easier to inspire with imagery related to human prey. Live actors portraying college students engaging in drunken revelry consistently rank as the most motivating stimuli, raising the average watts up to 400 per zombie as long as the actors were shown. Of course, this presents its own problems, as the actors often express concerns about staying in character while chained-up, flesh-eating zombies only meters away struggle in vain to devour them alive.

Unfortunately, while the Dead Run power station has led to many important insights into zombie behavior and physiology, it is simply too inefficient at the time of this writing to replace current power sources. The start-up costs are quite high, due to high safety and training requirements required by law for using the undead, while the profit per zombie is quite minimal. Furthermore, many people take a "not in my backyard" approach to such facilities, even though the risk is far lower than living near a nuclear power plant. This is complicated by the limited breakout at Dead

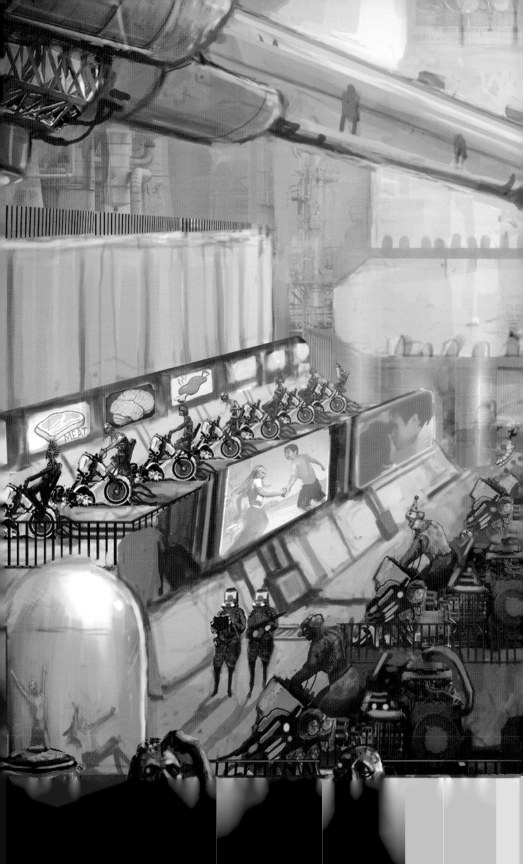

Run in the first year of its operation. A dozen undocumented workers were killed by a loose Revenant before the situation could be contained. Top management was charged with breaking federal labor and safety laws, and the station was relocated to Albania. Because of this incident, it is highly unlikely that similar power stations will replace traditional coal or nuclear plants anytime soon, although some believe that isolated locations could benefit from zombie-kinetic generated electricity.

Eventually, scientists hope to learn how to harness the *Omega Anima* directly in order to create necro-electric power plants, extracting the energy from zombie tissue and converting it into electricity. Futurists believe that within 50 years, necro-electric power will become one of the world's primary power sources; one that is safe and ecologically sound.

Medical Research

The zombie is traditionally thought of as harbinger of doom; one would not normally consider them the source of a cure for cancer or any other deadly disease. Yet, their amazing resilience has brought the undead to the attention of the medical community. Several efforts around the world are underway to derive medical applications from the undead. Most efforts are focused on zombies' immunity to cancer.

We know from extensive experimentation that zombies are immune to cancer. During the Cold War, researchers on both sides of the Iron Curtain tested the effects of radiation on the undead, as part of larger studies to determine the possible benefits of weaponizing certain zombie species. The undead developed radiation burns but did not suffer from radiation poisoning, even with prolonged exposure to massive doses of radiation. Furthermore, they did not develop tumors or any form of cancer.

Baffled by these results, scientists began to study zombies and cancer. They used a wide variety of carcinogens and even surgically inserted cancerous tumors in order to induce cancer in their test subjects. To their amazement, not a single zombie became ill. The genes of the zombie are incredibly durable and virulent. They resist mutation and no outside force, from radiation to carcinogenic chemicals, has managed to affect a zombie's genes. Even inserting cancerous tissue from living creatures does not sicken the zombie. Instead, the tissue is absorbed by the zombie.

Above: Artist's conception of a future power plant. Once scientists learn how to tap into the undead directly, there is no telling what we could accomplish.

Great strides have been made in this field, yet current research is held up by government regulations. Scientists now think that zombie stem cells are the key to unlocking the cure for cancer and many other diseases. These cells are the link between full zombie cells and human cells and contain traits of the living and undead. Theoretically, zombie stem cells could wipe out cancer in a human patient if properly administered and controlled with proper medication. In order to determine the proper procedure for treatment, researchers would need large quantities of zombie stem cells, but a shortage has held up research.

The most valuable zombie stem cells are found in the youngest undead, such as those just bitten by a Common Gray Shambler. Unfortunately, legislators have banned the creation or harvest of zombie stem cells on zombies less than a year old, stating that it could lead to unethical business practices, such as purposely transforming humans into Gray Shamblers to harvest their stem cells. Of course, this is to hide the real agenda of those who believe that the only good zombie is a dead zombie. They hide behind superstition instead of embracing research that could benefit all of humanity.

Zombie Intelligence & Domestication Studies

Typically stereotyped as mindless predators, few realize the intelligence lurking in the mind of the zombie, but time and again, the undead have proven to be far more cunning than previously suspected. In fact, some species possess near-human or even above-human intelligence and can communicate through speech or sign language. The field of zombie cognitive studies has only been recognized as a formal academic discipline for a few years now.

NANRI leads the field with its world-renowned Mummy Sign Language program, unique in the world for actually establishing prolonged communication with a mummy. Established by Dr. Linda Hasting, the program revived an ancient Egyptian Mummy nicknamed Freedom with a rejuvenating lotion infused with tanna leaf extract.

Once conscious, the mummy was taught sign language through the efforts of Dr. Hasting and her staff, despite Freedom's attempts to strangle them. Eventually, the mummy began to communicate in sign language. At first, Freedom only communicated through threats and insults.

Above: The Egyptian Mummy named Freedom was first noted when Colonel Kilgore of the British Navy gave the mummy to President Polk at a treaty signing in 1803. He remained in storage until NANRI found him and decided to use him as the first test subject of the Mummy Sign Language Program.

Dr. Hasting explained in an interview: "The undead seem to view the world much more negatively than the living. I stopped teaching any word with a negative connotation." After adjusting the lessons, Freedom has opened up and revealed much about itself. To learn more about Freedom and the NANRI Mummy Sign Language Program, read Dr. Hasting's book *The Wisdom of the Mummy: Talking with the Undead.*

Many people wonder why we should even bother to study the intelligence of the undead or try to communicate with them. These critics fail to grasp the practical applications of this knowledge, namely their utility as servants and workers. The more cognitive ability the undead possess, the more we can employ them. Fortunately, some researchers have made great strides by studying this topic. In fact, this is one of the most researched subjects in all areas of zombie studies. The Domesticated Gray Shambler has been recognized as a separate species. Due to labor laws in the USA and Europe, domesticated zombies can't be used for most jobs they are qualified to perform; however, corporate trials underway in Mexico, China, and Brazil show promising results.

Longevity & Immortality Through Partial Zombification

The goal of scientists is the discovery of a way to utilize the *Omega Anima* to extend human life span, possibly even achieve immortality. While this may seem unlikely, it should be possible given the mutability of the *Omega Anima* as it empowers many species with wildly different characteristics. For example, the Nukekubi and North American Cabin Lurker can actually levitate, a phenomenon still unexplained by science, while the Revenant is motivated by revenge, a social construct that has no basis in any ecosystem. The lesson being: when it comes to zombies, all bets are off. Once we understand the *Omega Anima*, it should be easy to determine how it gives zombies immortality. From that point, we should be able to use it to extend our lives, if not grant immortality. The futurist Allen Liddell has described what our future could look like:

"At first glance, the Smith family seems no different from the average American family of today. Mother has just gotten home from grocery shopping. The kids are playing on the front lawn with Spot and Rascal, the family dog and cat. Grandpa sits on the front porch, just enjoying the good

weather. Father takes a power nap on a hammock. But this is where the similarities between present and future end. Mother can't carry all the groceries by herself, so her domesticated zombie servant helps her. Like all zombie servants, it has cybernetic inhibitor implants to ensure it won't act up. Spot and Rascal both died – Spot to a passing car and Rascal due to a nasty hairball – but thanks to cyber-zombification, they are as good as new and will be faithful friends for decades to come. Even Grandpa enjoys the benefits of cyber-zombification. He's over 120 years old, yet his mind is as sharp as ever, and the only drawback is a slight gray pallor. Father enjoys a nice cold lemonade served by his personal cyber-zombie servant. And don't forget that the weather is now nice because of the clean green energy generated from *Omega Anima* power plants."

Above: The home of the future, all made possible by advances in zombie research. Clean power, longer life spans, and reliable domestic help are only some of the possibilities.

BIBLIOGRAPHY

Balfour, Francis. *Raise the Dead: A Secret History of Project RESURRECTIONIST.* 1st ed. Chicago: Gray Frog Inc., 1994. Print.

Hasting, Linda. *The Wisdom of the Mummy: Talking with the Undead.* Boston: North American Necrological Research Institute, 2006. Print.

Hill, Dorothy. *The Battle of New York City: The 1987 Zombie Riots.* 4th ed. New York: North American Necrological Research Institute, 2004. Print.

Jun-fan, Lee. *The Tao of Jiang-Shi-Do* . San Francisco: Knight Errant Press, 1977. Print

Junzt, Fran Von. *Hades at our Doorstep: The Undead and Mythology.* Rev. ed. . New York: Golden Goblin, 1952. Print.

Junzt, Heidi Von. *Birth from Death: The Necrogenesis Theory.* Expanded Ed. 2 vols. New York: Golden Goblin, 1965. Print.

I Touched A Zombie: A Tactile Identification Guide To North American Zombies. Dir. Tim Carpenter. North American Necrological Research Institute: 1985, Videocassette.

Quine, Anthony. *The Abattoir.* 1st ed. Chicago: Peterson Publishing, 1906. Print.

Shrewsbury, Laban. *Accounts of Revenant Excursions.* 2nd ed. 3 vols. London: The Royal Society, 1739. Print.

The Silens Domesday: A Complete Translation. 5th ed. Anthony Walker. Oxford: Octopus Classics, 1988. Print.

Winters-Hall, Edward. *Cuneiform Fragments from Ancient Sumer.* 1st ed. New York: Golden Goblin, 1908. Print.

Know Your Zombies!

Learning to identify which zombie species is which can be hard. Many of them have similar appearances, but a trained expert can distinguish between a harmless Dancing Zombie and a deadly North American Cabin Lurker.

We've created a learning aid to help you memorize the names and appearances of the 20 most prominent species of zombie in the world. This 18x24 poster lists the common and scientific names, along with a brief description for each species.

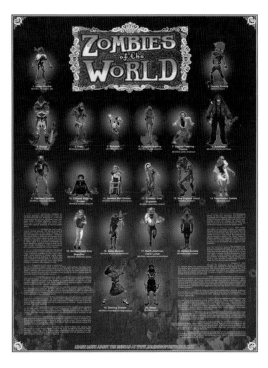

More dangerous than any zombie...

Zombie attacks happen all the time, but the undead are not the greatest threat in these events. Humans pose a greater danger to each other than any zombie, as panic, hysteria, and paranoia work through terrified survivors.

This 11x17 poster lists the type of survivors whom you should avoid in a zombie attack. Trusting one of them can be more lethal than a horde of hungry undead.

All these posters and more for sale at

zombiesoftheworld.com

Email sales@zombiesoftheworld.com for wholesale prices.